Y0-GMY-186

GOD SQUAD

Books by Walter Wagner

God Squad
Money Talks
God's Prison Gang (with Chaplain Ray)
Beverly Hills: Inside the Golden Ghetto
Heavenly Humor
You Must Remember This: Oral Reminiscences of the Real Hollywood
Solomon in All His Glory (Novel)
The Trip Beyond (with Brian Ruud)
To Gamble, or Not to Gamble
The Trouble with Wall Street (with Lewis A. Bracker)
The Man from Miracle Valley (with Don Stewart)
Turned on to Jesus (with Arthur Blessitt)
Born to Lose, Bound to Win (with A. A. Allen)
The Chaplain of Bourbon Street (with Bob Harrington)
The Golden Fleecers

GOD SQUAD

by Walter Wagner

A DOUBLEDAY-GALILEE ORIGINAL

DOUBLEDAY & COMPANY, INC., GARDEN CITY, NEW YORK 1979

IMPERIAL PUBLIC LIBRARY
P.O. BOX 307
IMPERIAL, TEXAS 79743
75

ISBN: 0-385-12802-9
Library of Congress Catalog Card Number 77–80918
Copyright © 1979 by Walter Wagner
All Rights Reserved
Printed in the United States of America
First Edition

For Rosemarie Paris, Ed McQueen
and the extraordinary men and women
of the God Squad.

CONTENTS

Make a chain: for the land is full of bloody crimes, and the city is full of violence.

—EZEKIEL 7:23

GOD SQUAD

CHAPTER 1

"If I Get Shot, I Get Shot"

Under the gray, leaden Detroit sky, the smell of death hovered like an avenging angel. The dark angel's grasp would shortly reach for two men who did not know each other—one a crusading minister, the other a deeply troubled Vietnam veteran.

Giant patches of snow were still splattered along the streets from last night's ferocious ice storm as Reverend William A. Paris pulled into the parking lot of his church a few minutes before noon on March 3, 1976. Fifty-two years old, he was a slim 145-pound man with an oval, handsome, and serene face. He wore a mustache, eyeglasses, a clerical collar, and more often than not a tranquil smile. He was quick to laugh, slow to anger.

Through the window of the church office, Reverend Paris' secretary noted his arrival. "Good," she sighed aloud. She had a long list of calls for him to return. There were, as always, parishioners with problems, there were sick calls to make, and then there were arrangements to be made for the funeral on Saturday for Mrs. Paris' cousin. Finally, there were longstanding arrangements to be made for the Parises' vacation in Hawaii, their first holiday in years.

Reverend Paris' secretary watched with surprise when, after a long moment, he failed to emerge from his car. He sat frozen behind the steering wheel of his new Cadillac. Suddenly he backed up, gunned the motor, and drove off, the snow parting like the Red Sea before the tires of the powerful automobile.

Inside the Cadillac, Bill Paris had heard a distress call on his police radio . . . "Barricaded gunman at the Addison Hotel. Suspect has already shot one man. He is armed and dangerous. Proceed with caution."

Bill Paris, the serene pastor, was answering the call. But why? Why should a minister respond to a police emergency? The role of a cleric, everyone knew, was passive rather than active. The police had their job and clergymen had their role. The role of a minister was to tend to the needs of his parishioners and the needs of God in the fortress of the pulpit and in the quiet surroundings of his office. But, Bill Paris thought, God at this moment was needed at the Addison Hotel.

God, no doubt, was waiting at the hotel, but so was the avenging angel.

Bill Paris ran several red lights on his way to the police hotspot. There wasn't a moment to lose . . .

The pretty, brown-eyed, copper-skinned girl from Maryland and the ebony-complected, freshly graduated seminarian had been introduced by mutual friends in New York in 1958. Their relationship ripened quickly. Young, they spoke readily, easily, idealistically of their dreams. Their lives were to be dedicated to service for others.

"I want to spend my life just being a good pastor," Bill Paris told Rosemarie. "I'm in love with you, Rose, and I'm in love with the Lord and I'm in love with people."

Without fussing or complaining, Rose would patiently wait for Bill when he was late for a date, which was often. He would arrive, his ubiquitous grin flashing, and explain that he had led a teenager to the Lord or had counseled friends who were having marital difficulties.

Rose had grown up thinking she would be a nurse. Although her family was religious, she never dreamed she would fall in love with and marry a pastor. A doctor, perhaps, but never a pastor. She had always planned to follow her parents advice. "Marry a good provider," they had told her repeatedly. Now she was committing herself to a young paladin of the pulpit about to assume his first pastorate in Riverhead, Long Island. His salary would be twenty-five dollars a month.

Bill Paris' all-black denomination—the African Methodist Episcopal Zion Church—had deep roots in American history. In 1796, a group of black members, dissatisfied with the limitations of segregated church life, withdrew from the John Street Methodist Church in New York City, and organized a church of their own which they named Zion. For a time, they maintained co-operative relationships with the white Methodist church. By 1821, however, the Zion church joined with representatives from other black congregations and formed themselves into the African Methodist Episcopal Zion Church.

They grew very little prior to the Emancipation Proclamation. After that, however, they burgeoned rapidly. Through the years, the denomination built 4,583 churches and a seminary; maintained a program of foreign-mission work in Africa, South America, and the West Indies; and played a large part in black cultural and educational development.

The church also was in the forefront of the expanding black civil rights movement at the time Bill and Rose Paris went to serve their first congregation in Long Island. As with most other denominations, the AME Zion Church was well-supported in some cities; in other cities it struggled for existence.

Bill and Rose struggled at Riverhead. It was a small, poor pastorate. But the lack of money never troubled Bill Paris. Simply, firmly, convincingly, he told Rose: "The Lord will provide for our needs."

And his unquestioning faith had worked. Usually they were dead broke. If they managed to get a few dollars ahead, Bill, more often than not, would give the money to a needy member of his flock. But, miraculously, the Lord always provided, as Bill Paris knew He would. A bag of groceries would appear on their doorstep, enough food for a week, from an anonymous donor. Or a parishioner would pump Bill's hand in gratitude for some favor. When Bill opened his hand, there would be a ten- or twenty-dollar bill.

Saying "I never meet any man as a stranger," Bill made deep, lasting friendships as he was transferred to churches in Newbury and Cambridge, Massachusetts, back to Riverhead, then to Plainville, Connecticut. In those years, two children, Stephen and Patricia, were born and Rose busied herself with raising her son and daughter and being a good parson's wife.

In the late sixties, Bill was transferred again, to Gary, Indiana, the two-fisted steel town on the shores of Lake Michigan. Here Bill began to thrive and flower as never before.

Working tirelessly, he built his congregation from sixty to two hundred. It was an event when Bill preached, his big, baritone voice cascading through the small church, inveighing against hatred and violence. He preached Jesus and he preached the message of Jesus—peace. Surprisingly, for a small man, his booming baritone carried above all the other voices in the congregation, particularly when his favorite hymn, "Bright Side," was part of the service.

By now the devastating riots in Watts, Detroit, and Newark had already occurred. In Gary too, young, tough, militant blacks were crying aloud, "Burn, Baby, Burn." Bill Paris preached his heart out in opposition. "Build, Baby, Build" and "Play it cool, play it smart," he told the young militants as he went out into the streets to meet them on their own turf. He counseled patience, and deliverance through the system, imperfect as it was. No black riot broke out in Gary, and many said that Bill Paris was as responsible for that as any man in the city.

But Gary did not completely escape violence. The harsh, cacophonous sound of teen-age motorcycle gangs began to be heard in the streets. Sputtering noise, mischief, and mayhem, the bikers held some parts of the city in terror. There were almost round-the-clock arrests for vandalism, drunkenness, and traffic congestion. Sometimes it became more serious, when the gangs would engage in robbery or rape. Then there were the deadly occasions when a member of a white biker gang would kill a black biker, or vice versa.

Bill Paris began a ministry among the bikers, relating to them whether they were black or white. He defused a number of tense situations; in one instance he talked the leaders of opposing biker gangs out of confronting one another in a "war." Soon he was known to bikers and the police as "The Hoodlum Priest." He became the official chaplain of the Gary Police Department, but spent most of his time in the streets, putting his faith to work. Where there was hatred, he talked of love; where there was anger, he spoke of goodwill; where there was defeat, he showed the path to victory. Most of all, Bill Paris was continuously visible in the crime-ridden parts of the city. As did Christ, he walked among sinners. Wherever there was trouble, there was his pulpit.

Bill Paris had assumed the activist mantle of a new breed of clergyman emerging in America. In Riverside, California; Albuquerque; Kansas City, Kansas; Minneapolis; Charlotte, North Carolina, and in dozens of other cities, men of the cloth were aggressively engaged in street and slum ministries. They rode in police cars, carrying Bibles instead of guns. They were guerrilla fighters for the Lord. It was a new action focus for these clergymen who courted trouble instead of waiting for trouble to find them. Their service was nondenominational, voluntary, unpaid. Their only reward was, as Bill Paris had told Rose, in being "a good pastor." But now their pastorate was an entire city, and anyone with a problem was a member of their congregation.

Someone, in one of the cities where such chaplains were serving, had nicknamed them "The God Squad." The name stuck.

Bill Paris' last transfer came in 1970, to Detroit, a city that most clerics attempted to avoid, if possible. Detroit had a ferocious reputation, well-deserved. The number-one urban battleground in the country, it had the nation's highest murder rate, and five hundred calls to the undermanned police tumbled in every hour to the central communications system at 1300 Beaubein Street.

When the Detroit assignment came, Bill Paris didn't feel threatened, discouraged, or afraid. He accepted the transfer as a challenge. He longed to be where the action was, and there was no doubt that Detroit, particularly the inner city where he would be located, offered action.

There were less than two hundred parishioners on the rolls when Bill Paris, Rose, and the children arrived. The Parises settled in and had no difficulty adjusting or accommodating themselves. Bill's church grew quickly and impressively under the force of his evangelical leadership. In three years the congregation tripled, to more than six hundred members.

In addition to building his flock and caring for his parishioners, Bill Paris became possessed, possessed by the notion that Detroit needed a God Squad. "I don't know any city that needs it more," he told Rose. Based on his experience in Gary, he knew what a chaplain corps could accomplish. If one minister in Gary could cut a measurable swath, then what could a larger force achieve? How many lives could be patched and sutured? How many might be won to God?

At last, in 1973, the objections of police brass, who regarded Bill Paris' idea to form a God Squad as "meddlesome" and "dangerous," were overcome by his persistence. Bill Paris and a handful of other ministers were given the go-ahead to form a corps.

"The purpose of the Chaplain Corps of the Detroit Police Department is to provide assistance of a religious and spiritual nature to the members of the Department and the people they serve at the precinct level," Bill Paris wrote in defining the God Squad's mission in the Motor City. Actually, Bill Paris had underdefined the role of the Corps. The Detroit God Squad would do much more than provide religious and spiritual assistance.

Under Bill Paris' leadership, the Squad became the largest chaplain corps in the country. There were thirty-nine members, including two women. Twenty-one in the Corps were black, eighteen were white. They were a hard-hitting, dedicated group filled with pride of accomplishment. Being a minister or a priest was not an automatic qualification for membership in the Corps. Clergymen who hadn't the right "feel" for the work or didn't achieve a quick understanding of the nature of police business were quietly but ruthlessly weeded out during the training program.

Every time a member of the Corps rode a shift in a two-officer patrol car, he was placing his life in jeopardy. In three years there had been many close calls, but no member of the God Squad had been killed—at least not yet . . .

The scene at the Addison Hotel was bedlam. More than one hundred uniformed policemen, including Chief Philip Tannian, had the place surrounded by the time Bill Paris arrived, less than fifteen minutes after he had heard the distress call in the parking lot of his church.

Siren wails ricocheted off the chill March air. Sawhorse barricades were already in place on the sidewalk adjoining the hotel, to keep back the large crowd that was forming. Several ambulances and fire trucks wheeled up. Sharpshooters from the Police Department's Tactical Services unit, similar to a swat squad, were scrambling to positions in windows and on rooftops near the Addison.

But for all the power at their disposal, the quick, heavy show of force, the efficiency of the response, the police were stymied, helpless. The gunman was still holed up inside the hotel, firing his rifle at policemen who came in range. The police fired back, but the gunman hadn't been hit.

Flashing his gold God Squad badge, Bill Paris walked to the center of the action, at the entrance to the hotel.

"He's been in there for about an hour," Lieutenant Kenneth Borieo told Bill Paris. "We've tried everything we know to get him out. So far, no luck. It's a stalemate."

The Addison had a reputation as a "shooting gallery"—a hotel that catered to narcotics users. Located in the heart of the inner city at Charlotte and Woodward, it was owned by fifty-two-year-old Harry Zartarian, who had unknowingly instigated the incident.

Several officers told Bill Paris what had happened. Shortly before noon, Zartarian had gone to the second-floor room of the gunman, who as yet was unidentified, and let himself in with his passkey. Told that 11 A.M. was checkout time, the man had responded by picking up a rifle and shooting Zartarian in the chest. Zartarian had staggered downstairs to the desk, bleeding profusely, and gasped for his clerk to call an ambulance and police. Zartarian had been taken to Detroit General Hospital and was in critical condition.

The gunman had bolted from the room and was ensconced in a sixth-floor stairwell, which led to the roof. Police had tried but failed to talk him down. They hadn't used gas canisters, fearing there might be others trapped in the hotel.

Bill Paris reacted immediately.

"I'm going up there," he told the knot of officers.

"It's too dangerous," one of the policemen said.

Standing there, they heard the sound of gunfire from inside the hotel.

"You've tried guns and shooting," Bill Paris said. "Now let's try God."

None of the policemen wanted to argue with the firmness in Bill Paris' voice.

"If you have to go up," one said, "at least put on a bulletproof vest."

Calmly, Bill Paris said, "No. If I get shot, I get shot."

Bill Paris walked up to the sixth-floor stairwell and into another group of officers who were wearing gas masks. Fifteen of them were keeping the gunman at bay. One policeman darted from cover and let go a shot. It missed.

"Just a minute," Bill told the officers. "Let me talk to him."

The policemen gaped at the minister. They also attempted to convince Bill Paris that it was too dangerous. But he remained firm.

"Hold your fire," he said, and in the silence the big baritone voice of Bill Paris boomed up to the gunman.

"Hey, buddy, let's talk this over. I'm a chaplain—I'm not a policeman. I'll take off my coat to show you I'm unarmed." He paused. There was no reply. Then: "You can't get out. But I'll personally guarantee you won't get hurt. Can I come up?"

In a low, clear voice the gunman called, "Okay."

Bill Paris removed his jacket and said a quick, silent prayer as he readied himself for the confrontation.

Outside the hotel, the crowd of more than two hundred onlookers was growing restive, spoiling for a victim. The crowd was mean, sullen, combative. It was the sort of ugly crowd that would have cried "Jump" if there had been a potential suicide on the hotel roof. In the midst of the roiling mob, hawkers of hypodermic needles had appeared and were doing a gold-rush business among those onlookers who were heroin addicts.

The gray, leaden sky now had flecks of blue. Probably it wouldn't snow again. But under the sky, the avenging angel still waited as Bill Paris turned the corner and began to climb the stairs. The first thing he saw was a .22-caliber rifle aimed directly at his head.

CHAPTER 2

A Time to Die

The man holding the .22 had short, muscle-rippled arms laced with needle tracks. Of medium height, stocky, and wearing his hair in Afro-style, Chauncey West, Jr., hadn't been the same since he'd returned from Vietnam in 1969. Discharged from the Army with a 70 per cent disability pension, Chauncey, now twenty-eight years old, had found furies in himself that he was powerless to control. The anger and hatred that overwhelmed him had led to his being hospitalized sixteen times at veterans and state institutions for depression and for drug and alcohol abuse.

"He wasn't wounded in combat," his younger brother, James F. West, said. "The only thing wounded was his mind. It all started after he came out of the Army. He would be in fine shape for a while after coming back from the hospital, then he would go into a trance."

A cousin, Victor K. Brown, recalled that Chauncey would often just sit quietly "and then start to cry." Mrs. Erma West said she hadn't given up hope for her son. "I felt he would be all right."

Despite the emotional turbulence seething within him, Chauncey seemed to be functioning well enough most of the time. He worked as a welder at Chrysler's Mack Avenue stamping plant, and had saved enough money to buy a house and a car.

But he couldn't stay away from drugs, which seemed to exacerbate his short temper. After one bout with heroin, he was arrested on May 15, 1975, for shooting a friend in the stomach with a shotgun. The quarrel had begun over a girl. The friend recovered, and

Chauncey was charged with assault with intent to murder. Despite the serious charge, he was freed, pending trial. That was only the first of a number of mistakes committed by judicial and psychiatric authorities in the torturous trail that resulted in the shootout at the Addison Hotel.

Six weeks after the shotgun episode, Chauncey quarreled with a neighbor. Bystanders separated the two men. Chauncey went home for a fix, and an hour later he set his neighbor's house on fire. He was arraigned on two counts of arson and ordered to undergo psychiatric evaluation at a Detroit mental health clinic.

Chauncey was twice examined by psychiatrists. The first time the doctors said he was competent to stand trial for both the shooting and arson incidents. But the second time the doctors reversed themselves and said he was incompetent to go to trial.

Faced with conflicting expert opinions, Judge Robert Colombo ordered Chauncey to the Center for Forensic Psychiatry at Ypsilanti State Hospital for further evaluation and treatment.

Chauncey spent six weeks at the Forensic Center. By September 3, the doctors there had concluded that he could in fact stand trial. Chauncey was then transferred to the Wayne County jail.

The arson case was tried first, on September 18. Judge Colombo found Chauncey innocent by reason of insanity. Then the judge again ordered Chauncey to the Forensic Center for still more evaluation, and postponed for sixty days the trial on the shooting charge.

After spending another month and a half at the Ypsilanti facility, Chauncey was discharged as sane. Doctors ruled he didn't meet the criteria to be kept in the hospital—in effect, that he was not mentally disturbed to the extent that required institutional care. Chauncey walked out a free, unmolested man. The only condition of his release was a promise to continue treatment at the Kirwood Mental Health Center in Detroit. There is no record that Chauncey ever appeared for a single treatment at Kirwood; nor did the Center at Ypsilanti check on the status of Chauncey's follow-up treatment in Detroit.

Still facing the intent-to-murder charge, Chauncey should have been arrested the day he was discharged from the Forensic Center.

But it didn't happen, because of bureaucratic snafus, misunderstandings, and inefficient paperwork. It was a critical lapse. If Chauncey had been taken into custody that day, the ensuing events at the Addison Hotel would not have occurred.

The Detroit police said they were not notified of Chauncey's discharge from the Forensic Center. The Center said it did notify the Wayne County prosecutor's office. But Richard J. Padzieski, deputy chief of the prosecutor's criminal division, said his office files showed no record of any notification from the Center that Chauncey West had been released.

For his part, William H. Meyer, acting director of the Center, said that neither the court nor the prosecutor ever informed the Center that Chauncey West was a suspect in a murder case.

"We were given no reason to believe that this man was dangerous, or that any charge was pending against him," Meyer said.

Thus, the human time bomb named Chauncey West, Jr., was prowling Detroit when he should have been in a hospital room or a prison cell.

On Tuesday, March 2, 1976, Chauncey was at his mother's home. About 11 P.M. he said he was leaving to see a couple of friends. But when Mrs. West saw him start out the door with a rifle he had purchased at a department store a month earlier, she tried to stop him. "He wouldn't listen," Mrs. West said. Until tonight, Chauncey had stored the rifle at his mother's place. But now he wanted it with him.

After making it through the ice storm, Chauncey, by 11:30 P.M., had checked into the Addison Hotel. If the clerk noticed the cased rifle, he said nothing. At the Addison no questions were asked about luggage.

By 11:45, heroin was swimming through Chauncey's body. At that same moment, Bill Paris was preparing to go to bed. Neither man could know they would meet the next day—explosively—in the sixth-floor stairwell of the Addison.

Their meeting only lasted for an instant.

Though Chauncey had said he would talk to Bill Paris, the moment he saw the minister attempting to climb the stairwell, he fired his .22. Bill Paris' foot never reached the second step. He took the bullet square in the forehead from a distance of less than ten feet.

"Oh, my God," a nearby officer screamed as Bill Paris reeled back in agony. Because Bill Paris was still exposed, twenty-five-year-old Officer Martin G. Fuhrmann volunteered to pull him to safety. Perhaps he was still alive. To cover Officer Fuhrmann, Inspector Robert M. Porte ordered smoke and tear-gas grenades tossed up the stairwell.

Inching along the narrow corridor like a combat infantryman, Officer Fuhrmann reached Bill Paris, stood up, lifted the minister in his arms, and was making his way back to cover when a bullet from Chauncey's rifle drilled through his gas mask near his right eye. He fell to the floor. Other officers then pulled the two wounded men out of the line of fire.

Bill Paris and Officer Fuhrmann, both bleeding, were rushed down the stairs. As they were carried into the street in sight of the crowd, many of the spectators gave the clenched-fist "black power" salute. The crowd clapped, laughed, cheered, jeered, hooted, and shouted obscenities.

"The only reason they are jeering the chaplain is that they think he's a cop," a disgusted policeman said. "I'd like to throw up."

Chauncey West had now shot three men, and at the moment no one knew if any of them would survive.

Despite the smoke and tear gas engulfing Chauncey from the grenades, he wasn't ready to give up. There was still a way to escape, he thought. He bashed the butt of his rifle against the skylight at the top of the stairwell. Climbing through the shattered glass, he made it to the roof and hid behind a shed. For a minute or two, he hungrily breathed the fresh air. Then he peered from behind the shed, trying to determine his next move.

On the roof of another hotel, three hundred yards away, Sergeant William Wurm, a trained anti-sniper expert, aimed and fired his 30.06-caliber weapon. The single shot tore through Chauncey West's chest. The furies inside him were silent now, and the avenging angel had its first victim.

Shortly after Chauncey West's death, the ambulances carrying

Bill Paris and Officer Fuhrmann reeled to a stop outside the emergency room of Detroit General. Both men were fighting for their lives.

As word of what had happened to Bill Paris at the Addison Hotel spread around the city, a swarm of colleagues from the God Squad, policemen, family, and friends gathered at the hospital for what they all feared was a deathwatch.

Looking numb, Rose Paris arrived with her children. "Bill's in the hands of God," was all she could say to those who offered sympathy, hope, and encouragement.

"Bill Paris and I have discussed the heroics of chaplains," Officer Edward McQueen, the Police Department's co-ordinator of the Chaplain Corps, said to a friend. "He doesn't believe in heroics, he just believes in doing his job.

"Bill Paris has always been able to talk himself out of any situation. He had no doubt he could talk that gunman down. He's a superaggressive guy. He's not afraid of anything. He's a leader," McQueen concluded.

Two higher-ranking policemen recalled other occasions when Bill Paris had responded to emergencies.

The previous December, Inspector John May remembered, a police officer named George Weary III, who was twenty-nine years old, had killed himself and his wife.

"Bill helped us break the news to Weary's mother. Without Bill there, we would have been lost. He took over completely.

"Bill is a guy who's difficult to turn around. He's a fine man. But the trouble, perhaps, with the chaplains is that they have blind faith and they do things even policemen wouldn't."

Joseph Areeda, now deputy police chief, talked about a recent narcotics bust on the east side while he was commander of the 5th Precinct. It was one o'clock in the morning, but when he phoned Bill Paris, Bill was there in eighteen minutes. Areeda clocked him.

A taut situation had developed after the officers rushed into the house. A woman who was present toppled over and died without anyone touching her.

"The circumstances of the woman's death were strange and unusual," Areeda said. "An autopsy later showed she died of an acute liver disorder, but there was a potentially ugly situation developing. Her friends were blaming us for her death. After Bill arrived, he got everyone to calm down. I don't know what might have happened, but nothing did happen, because of Bill."

Eighteen hours after they arrived at the hospital, the band of well-wishers heard the first news from the doctors. Harry Zartarian was in serious but stable condition. The hotelkeeper was certain to recover. Officer Fuhrmann's right eye had been removed and damage to his temple repaired. He would recover too. Bill Paris, however, was hooked to a life-support respirator. The bullet had been removed from his head, and he was holding on by a thread.

Pacing the hall, the Reverend Ernest C. Klein, pastor of Immanuel United Church of Christ and a member of the God Squad, said, "What Bill did in trying to help the gunman is not unusual for the Corps. All of us would have answered that call. It didn't require any great motivation; it is just part of our calling, which is to serve."

At 4:20 P.M., about fifty-three hours after Chauncey West had promised Bill Paris conversation and delivered lead, the respirator, barely sustaining the life of the founder of the Detroit God Squad, was turned off. The man who only wanted to be a good pastor was dead.

He was the first police chaplain in the nation killed in the line of duty.

The avenging angel had claimed its second victim.

CHAPTER 3

Aftermath of a Hero

Detroit cried.

Virtually everyone in the city mourned the death of the brave chaplain. The tragedy was especially unsettling because no one could explain it. How explain the bartering of an exemplary life for that of a murderous misfit?

There were a few exceptions to the citywide mood of grief: the cynical "A man's got to be a fool to walk in unarmed against a junkie with a rifle" and those who had cheered and hooted when Bill Paris was carried out of the Addison Hotel fatally wounded.

Dr. Bruce Danto, a psychiatrist, commenting on the grotesque emotions exhibited by the crowd, said such people viewed the world in terms of a power structure, with violence as the strongest motivating factor.

"They negate the power of human life. They identify with violence and disidentify with those attempting to support law and order.

"This is a frightening, tragic point of view. They are cheerleaders of violence and they are going to make us lose our society."

The city's two lively newspapers spewed out headlines of helpless anguish. "He Only Wanted to Save a Life," said the Detroit *News*. The *Free Press* declared: "Chaplain in Siege Dies—Hero Hailed."

Bill Paris was given a hero's burial, with full police honors. The memorial service was conducted at his own church. Mayor Coleman Young and Police Chief Tannian were there. So were hundreds of officers from the Detroit Police Department, many of whom had never met Bill Paris. Friends had come from Chicago, Pennsylvania, New York, Indiana, and South Carolina. Every member of the God Squad was present. The church was filled to overflowing, and loudspeakers piped the services to the throng outside.

There were more than a dozen eulogies, and for once the eulogies did not exaggerate and magnify the departed; rather, they accurately portrayed the life that Bill Paris had led.

No one was more articulate than Chief Tannian. "Bill Paris gave his life for a man he never saw or knew. He also gave it for the men and women of the Police Department."

Tannian, not without difficulty, looked directly at Rose Paris, who was sitting in the front pew with her children. She appeared stunned and wan. "We are better for knowing Bill," the chief concluded, "and we thank you for sharing him with us." His voice was choked with both frustration and reverence.

Mayor Young praised Bill Paris as "one of our greatest and strongest citizens. Every Detroiter today recognizes, in his life and in his manner of death, that the Reverend Paris has challenged us. He was actively trying to solve the city's problems. In his life, and even in his dying, Reverend Paris was issuing a challenge to us—to fight to keep this city alive."

Then the Reverend Charles Adams said: "You can shoot a man like that down, but you can never keep him down. Bill Paris saw violence and he tried to stop it. He is not a victim, but a victor. His courage is indestructible."

This was met by shouts of "Amen" and applause. The members of the AME Zion Church didn't believe in sad funerals . . . a man's passing from this life was but a step to paradise. "Bill Paris was as close to God as any man I ever met," the Reverend Adams added.

The chief eulogist was Bill Paris' longtime friend, AME Zion Bishop George J. Leake III of South Carolina. Perspiration dripping from his face, his eyes blazing, Bishop Leake made himself hoarse delivering an emotionally draining hour-and-a-half eulogy that was often punctuated by shouts and handclapping from the congregation.

There was a note of high surprise in Bishop Leake's peroration.

Bill Paris had visited him recently and talked about his death—as though, the bishop said, he had a premonition. Bill had said: "When I die, I want to know that my life has not been in vain. My only regret will be that I didn't have more to give and to share."

Nearing the end of his eulogy, the bishop said: "A man pulled a gun and killed Bill the other day. Bill didn't have to go up those stairs." A hush fell over the church and the only sound was the trailing echo from the loudspeakers. "But Bill did it to try and save another human being."

The bishop's final words were for the comfort of Rose Paris and her children.

"When death strikes suddenly, by some tragic, bewildering process, our minds question *why*. A multitude of questions involving the motive and ways of God surface in our minds.

"The death of Bill Paris has raised many difficult problems for this family to resolve. It is a fruitless inquiry. Clearly we do not know God's entire plan. But the promise is that one day we *shall* know and understand, even as God now understands us."

The entire assemblage, including Rose Paris, joined in the singing as the choir launched into Bill Paris' beloved hymn, "Bright Side."

The casket was then borne outside by a police honor guard, past Bill's assembled colleagues in the God Squad. As the funeral procession slowly made its way down Beachwood and onto Tireman, heading for the cemetery in suburban Wayne, thousands of onlookers in the streets watched respectfully. Two blue-and-white police helicopters flew overhead as the police band played. An hour later, Bill Paris was buried. The good pastor, who'd had a premonition of his death, had found rest.

Seven months later, Bill Paris was given a posthumous citation by the City Council, one of seventy-five awarded that day for outstanding police work. The citation commended him for his sacrifice beyond the call of duty. Some thought it in bad taste and a sign of quick forgetfulness that Bill Paris wasn't individually honored. Rose Paris accepted the honor, and, characteristically, made no complaint.

Also cited was Officer Fuhrmann. Sightless in one eye, he wore a black lens in half of his eyeglasses. Officer Fuhrmann hadn't yet returned to duty. "It's up to him," a police spokesman said. "Whenever he wants to come back, he's more than welcome."

As for Rose Paris, she still hasn't completely adjusted to widowhood. Looking remarkably young and attractive at forty-seven years of age, she sits in her small gray-brick house in an integrated neighborhood, a half hour's drive from downtown Detroit. An afternoon soap opera runs idly on the TV as she makes a visitor comfortable with homemade fruitcake and coffee in the yellow-draped living room strewn with ivy plants grown by her husband.

It's been more than two years since she buried her husband, but her memories of him are warm and alive. She still wears his wedding ring, and says the thought of remarriage has never crossed her mind.

Rose Paris earns a modest living, about $9,000 a year, as an interior decorator. When Bill died, the Police Department announced prematurely that his family qualified for the $10,000 lump-sum death payment officers' families receive, even though Bill was not formally a member of the Department.

The $10,000 payment was not forthcoming. Not that Rose Paris complains. She never worries about money, believing still in her husband's assurance that "God will provide." A Detroit service club sent her a check for $1,000 following Bill's death, and she receives a weekly stipend from the city of only $115, the official price in Detroit of a life given in sacrifice. She will receive the weekly check for nine years.

"You should really be talking to him," Rose Paris is saying, "because Bill just had a way with people. He was doing for them, every day, many, many things that I didn't even know about.

"Since his death, I've met many people who tell me that Bill helped them. I've gotten a lot of nice letters. Bill was just a person who knew about people."

Wearing a blue suit, yellow blouse, and tortoiseshell glasses, Rose Paris smiles. "We had a strange house. We always shared whatever we had, from food to clothing to money. This was a constant thing with us. We had a house where people just passed through freely. Some stayed overnight, some only for dinner. I would always have to put a little extra on because I never knew when he had somebody coming. There was nothing we had that he wouldn't give away. I have seen him without a penny, but, you know, if it was his last penny and someone wanted it, well, he would get that last penny."

Rose Paris suddenly segues into silence, and her face wears a slight frown. "You know," she says after a minute or two of reflection, "we are misled from the beginning. They say you get married and live happily ever after. But I know now that isn't true."

Her eye catches a frame or two of the onrushing soap opera, and her mood brightens. "Bill was like a doctor, always on call. One night, while we were eating dinner, he got a call to go out where there was a shooting. When he came back hours later, of course his appetite was gone. 'If only I could have talked to that man, maybe I could have stopped him,' he said. All he told me was that the man shot his wife and two children. He wouldn't say more. He used to say, 'If one of us has a load to carry, that's enough. It's not fair that both of us have to carry it.'"

Whenever there was a murder or suicide in his congregation, Bill would get upset. He would brood for days. He'd say, "They don't have to kill each other. They don't have to kill themselves. There's another way, there's a better way." Without irony, she adds that in the pulpit Bill often preached about the dignity of all human life in God's eyes and the tragedy of senseless killings.

"Yes," she says, "I miss him. Since he died, I've been in a shell. The last time I saw him was at breakfast that day—we always had breakfast together—and as he went out the door he said, as he always did, 'Rose, I love you.'"

That day, the day Bill was shot, Rose returned home at about 4:15 P.M. There were police cars in the driveway and several officers on the porch. Rose thought it was just one more routine meeting between Bill and members of the Department.

"There's been an accident. Your husband is hurt," one of the officers told Rose.

Nothing to worry about, Rose decided. An accident can be patched up.

"I think you'd better go with me to the hospital, Mrs. Paris," the officer added. "He's been shot."

"All those people at the hospital were talking to me, but I wasn't hearing what they were saying, because I had left him well and together, and now this. . . . It hadn't dawned on me that it was as bad as it was. It still hadn't dawned on me just what had happened or why all those people from the Police Department and the Chaplain Corps were there."

At last a woman neurologist came to her and said: "There are no vital signs of life. Your husband is gone."

"I didn't faint," Rose Paris remembers, "and I don't know why. I can't explain to you how I felt, or what I was thinking. I was just drowning, just lost in an endless sea.

"At the funeral I was floating along. I saw the hearse and all the people in the street. The shock of what had happened still hadn't hit me. I'm not sure the shock has hit me yet."

What does she think of the man who shot her husband? Was Chauncey West's life a fair trade for the life of Bill Paris?

She bristles and replies indignantly: "How can you ask me that! I don't think anything would be a fair trade for my husband's life. I know I am selfish, but I have to say that.

"The man who shot my husband was sick, and Bill was trying to reach out and help him. When the man told him he could come up and talk with him, Bill believed him. My husband always took a man's word.

"I have no ill feelings for the man, because he wasn't the one that shot my husband. The needle shot Bill. No one in his right mind would have killed Bill, and certainly no one who knew him would have killed Bill.

"The man is dead, and what good would it do to carry vengeance in my heart? What I would like to do is roll back the years and months so that the tragedy could have been avoided. I just wish it had never happened."

Rose Paris says she has all the newspaper stories about her husband's death, but she hasn't read them. "I don't want to read them. I have refused to read them."

By accident, she saw one story which showed a picture of Bill being carried from the Addison Hotel. "He was so lifeless. My husband was a proud man. He walked by himself. They wouldn't have had to carry him if he wasn't hurt bad. I saw that picture in the hospital and, seeing them carrying him, I knew the end was near."

Other than his gravestone, there is no memorial to Bill Paris in Detroit. What would make a fitting memorial to her husband's memory?

Rose Paris, three times a grandmother, pauses and reflects. Then she says: "Bill always thought it was necessary to have ministers available to help people in need. That's his memorial. The Chaplain Corps is what he'd like to be remembered for."

CHAPTER 4

No Phoenix from the Ashes

It is impossible to understand the mood, attitudes, fears and hopes of Detroit without recalling, however briefly, the six-day riot in July 1967.

The final casualty list stemming from the riot was 43 dead, 2,000 injured, 7,331 arrested, 5,000 homeless, 1,628 buildings gutted by fire, and $500 million in property damage.

The echoes of the riot will linger on for years—nothing in Detroit will be the same for at least a generation, and the process of rebuilding will take at least that long. The physical as well as the psychological damage done to Detroit by the riot was enormous.

More than a decade after the sundering riot, Detroit is still a city in tatters. Gutted buildings, rubble-strewn vacant lots, boarded-up houses, and shuttered stores are visible everywhere.

The most far-reaching result of the 1967 riot has been white flight. Raw, nerve-jangling fear of another riot, as well as the high incidence of crime in the inner city, drove the whites into the suburbs and decimated the large ethnic neighborhoods that once added immeasurably to what charm Detroit had. Before the riot, Detroit was the nation's fifth largest city. It is now the sixth. Population has dwindled to 1.3 million, a precipitous decline from 1.8 million in 1967. Thirty-five per cent of Detroit was black at the time of the riot; today Detroit is 60 per cent black, with the black majority growing.

The city is black-ruled. The mayor (Coleman A. Young), the new chief of police (William Hart), the county sheriff, the school superintendent, and seven of the thirteen members of the school board are black. None of these posts was held by a black in 1967. The only Detroit institution that is still white-dominated is the police force. Only 25 per cent of the 5,200-member Department is black. Even so, white officers have repeatedly complained, and the complaint has caused tension, that they were being passed over for promotions because priority was being given to blacks and the three hundred women on the force.

The Department adopted an affirmative-action program in 1974 in an effort not only to increase the number of blacks and women in police ranks, but to promote them faster. The major emphasis is on upgrading the black policeman. According to white officers, a black is often promoted ahead of a white policeman who has scored higher on a qualifying exam. Many white officers claim that they have been repeatedly passed over for advancement. The friction does little to improve the morale of the Department.

In July 1976, the city was staggering under a budget deficit of $103.3 million. Drastic steps, said Mayor Young, were needed to save money. A total of 241 firemen were laid off. The number of city workers was reduced from 23,677 to 18,403. Those cuts saved $46 million. Then the mayor, in order to save another $20 million, astonished and angered the city by announcing that 972 policemen, about one sixth of the force, was to be furloughed.

Terror swept the city. The chief of police said bravely that, despite the reductions, basic police services would not deteriorate. But his statement was challenged by skeptical police union officials, downtown businessmen, and outraged, frightened citizens. Police protection was already spread too thin—4.4 per 1,000. Those who opposed the police cuts were right. Crime went up immediately and alarmingly.

David Jones, a thirty-one-year-old mortgage company executive, was shot to death in a parking lot near Olympic Stadium. Police said the motive was robbery. The dead man, however, still had four dollars in his wallet. The killing of David Jones caused a furor in the city.

Though murder was rising in the city in the wake of the police cuts, it was an ugly incident at Cobo Hall, Detroit's cavernous arena located smack in downtown, that showed how close the city was to anarchy.

While two rock groups were performing at Cobo Hall on Sunday, August 15, 1976 (six weeks after the police firings), between two and three hundred black youths, members of gangs known as the Black Killers and the Errol Flynns, invaded the arena in which several thousand persons were seated. The gang youths, unopposed, beat people with chairs and robbed members of the audience at will. Only ten policemen were on duty at Cobo Hall. Vastly outnumbered, they refused to intercede. Nor did they call for back-up help. The Black Killers and the Errol Flynns were the masters of Cobo Hall.

Shortly, the gang violence spread outside the arena. More than twenty stores were robbed and looted (of cold cuts, cupcakes, beer, wine, and cigarettes) and a number of windows were smashed. Two women were raped. One, an eighteen-year-old girl from suburban Livonia, was stripped and assaulted in the thick of downtown, in front of the Pontchartrain Hotel, while her male companion looked on helplessly.

The next day, Deputy Mayor William Beckham, standing in for Mayor Young, who was vacationing in the Caribbean, ordered 450 laid-off officers back to immediate duty. A coalition of 250 Detroit businessmen demanded that Beckham declare a state of emergency and increase round-the-clock police patrols.

Two hundred and fifty of the newly rehired policemen were assigned to gang duty. A 10 P.M. curfew for those under eighteen was initiated.

"We're going to take the city back—beginning now," Beckham told Detroiters. "Someone's going to be hurt. Don't let it be your child. The city's crime problem is down to the bottom line, and it's a matter of applying pure law. In the language of the streets, we are prepared to 'get it on' with the gangs." Police patrols fanned across the city over the next twenty-four to forty-eight hours, arresting gang members involved in the attack at Cobo Hall.

Back from vacation, Mayor Young announced that he was calling in more than eighty state police troopers. They were assigned to cruise the city's sixty-two miles of freeways, where gangs were now assaulting and robbing disabled motorists. The state police contingent, the mayor said, freed more officers for street patrols and other crime-prevention duties.

Two weeks after the Cobo Hall incident, executive police duty officer Russell Gallaway said, after a personal tour of the city: "Everything seems fairly peaceful. From what I've seen, the gang situation is quiet. As long as we maintain our patrol effectiveness, we will maintain a decrease in gang activities."

Nevertheless, Boy Scouts of America executives canceled their convention in Detroit, citing downtown crime as the reason. Undaunted, the city-supported Department of Public Information was scouring the country for convention business. One ad in the New York *Times* said: "Detroit. A nice place to visit . . . and a great place to live!"

In April 1977, six Detroit teen-agers were put on trial, accused of raping the two women during the Cobo Hall rampage. Also put on trial the same month for the murder of David Jones was Rutherford Massenberg, a black seventeen-year-old picked up on an informant's tip.

In both cases, the defendants were found not guilty. A jury of eleven blacks and one white found the six alleged rapists innocent. A jury of eight blacks and four whites acquitted Massenberg, who was also awaiting trial on a charge of slaying a fifty-year-old fruit-stand operator in June 1976, after escaping from the Wayne County Youth Home.

Prosecutors in both cases were shocked at the verdicts. The cases were well-prepared, and in both instances there was eyewitness testimony. The Detroit *News* and many white Detroiters felt that the defendants had been freed solely because they'd been tried by predominantly black juries. Still, the *News* dealt gingerly with the issue. "Racial considerations sometimes seem to exert more influence than the evidence upon jury deliberations," the paper said in an editorial. These verdicts "have brought Detroit a new sense of helplessness in its struggle for order and justice. . . . Certainly a downtown revival in Detroit won't occur until a citizen can visit Olympic Stadium or Cobo Hall without fear of being raped or shot."

Both the Cobo Hall and Olympic Stadium cases remain unsolved, nor are they any longer being investigated by the Detroit Police Department.

Reacting sharply to claims that it was becoming increasingly difficult to convict blacks before Detroit juries, which usually are primarily black, Mayor Young said the charges were completely without foundation.

"If anyone thinks these verdicts will have any effect on our crime-prevention efforts," the mayor added, "I dare them to commit crimes. If they do, they will go to prison."

Detroit is feeding convicted criminals into the prison system so swiftly that a 3,000-bed shortage has developed in local penal institutions. Governor William G. Milliken has asked the state legislature to approve the immediate conversion of the Wayne County Child Development Center, a seminary, abandoned Kincheloe Air Force Base, and the downtown department-store warehouse of J. L. Hudson into state prisons and correctional facilities. No one doubts that the facilities are needed. Since the early 1970s, Detroit has been known as Murder Capital, U.S.A. The most lethal year was 1974, when a record 801 homicides were committed in the city, more than two a day. Detroit still has the highest homicide rate in the nation—49.3 murders for each 100,000 persons. (By comparison, the rate in New York is 20.5 murders for every 100,000 residents.)

The fact that the murder rate (as well as the rate for every other category of crime) remains high has ravaged the downtown Detroit landscape. By day, pedestrians walk warily. At night, downtown is a graveyard. The merchants in metropolitan Detroit estimate their aggregate shoplifting losses at more than $450,000 a day! As a direct result of the murder of David Jones, the management of Olympic Stadium announced its intention to build a new arena in Pontiac, outside the Detroit city limits. Several large hotels have closed in the past few years, and hundreds of merchants are fleeing the city each year, giving the visitor the unmistakable impression that Detroit is a burnt-out case.

Though businessmen and residents have been fleeing in panic to the northern and western suburbs for more than ten years, Henry

Ford II has decided to gamble that Detroit can be turned around. With $337 million contributed by Ford, General Motors, Allied Chemical, Amoco, Burroughs, Goodyear, Gulf and Western, Kresge, and other giant corporations, an impressive complex of four 39-story, octagonal office towers and the Detroit Plaza (at 73 stories, the world's tallest hotel) has been completed. The mammoth development is called the Renaissance Center and is a bold, expensive effort to revive downtown Detroit. However, it will be years before the Center can be judged a success or failure. The opening of the hotel in April 1977, did draw chartered busloads of curious suburbanites and a dental convention to ogle the hotel's overstated, gloppy eight-story atrium lobby replete with a half-acre lake, hanging plants, and gardens. But the suburbanites reboarded their buses for home, most before nightfall, and few of the dentists ventured out into the city.

The city's problems are so severe, if not terminal, that a single development, no matter how imposing, can't begin to right all that is wrong. The fundamental things that are wrong in Detroit are the continuing population decline, a lack of employment, inadequate housing, and inferior education.

"I can remember when this city was almost on the verge of having two million people, back in 1952 when I was in school writing civics papers," says Elliott S. Hall, a forty-year-old attorney. Hall and the city fathers have reconciled themselves to the fact that Detroit isn't likely ever to reach the two-million population figure, which means that the tax base continues to erode and that Detroit is becoming a city of the poor.

Widespread poverty in Detroit keeps the crime rate soaring. The Police Department's God Squad co-ordinator, Ed McQueen, who joined the force after the 1967 riot ("There had to be a better way"), says that the poor victimize the poor in Detroit—80 per cent of crime is committed by blacks against blacks.

Only the injection of a massive $3.4 billion in poverty and welfare funds by the federal government in the past decade has kept the city from crumbling. Though the automobile industry is still booming, there is a surplus of labor. Unemployment in the central city is 13.9 per cent. Overall, the city has a 10.4 per cent unemployment rate. Hardest hit are black teen-agers, who have a whopping out-of-work rate of 41 per cent.

Not long ago, 44,000 Chrysler workers were laid off because the company was suffering a temporary slump in sales. Fifty of the workers, their wives, and children held a memorial service for their jobs after they had been unemployed for five months.

It was a mock funeral, staged on April Fool's Day. But there was no joking, just the frustration of five months without a job, without a regular paycheck, and an uncertain future because supplemental pay benefits were about to expire.

"They'll give us our jobs back after we've lost everything," one man shouted. "They don't care."

One of the first things that happened when the layoff finally ended was that a long-frustrated black walked up to his white foreman and shot him three times. Though the murder was witnessed by dozens of assembly-line workers, no witnesses came forward. Chrysler promptly offered a $10,000 reward for information leading to the conviction of the slayer. The reward so far is uncollected.

It has been said of Detroit that it has more industry and less charm than any other American metropolis, and even without its high crime rate the city would not be regarded as one of the world's garden spots.

The quality of life is so restrictive that there is little to do except work hard or (for the unemployed) to prey on those who have jobs. As a result, vice in all its guises—drinking, gambling, prostitution, drugs—flourishes. There are more than 40,000 heroin addicts in Detroit, the highest per-capita ratio in the nation.

When the day's work is done, most Detroiters come home to vastly inadequate housing. The city's housing stock—it has more than 200,000 single-family homes, more than any other city in America—should be one of its greatest assets, but the deterioration that has blighted the inner city neighborhoods in New York, Chicago, and St. Louis has been even more pervasive in Detroit.

In part, the widespread deterioration has resulted from the 1967 riot and the fear it engendered. Another factor has been the federal government's unsuccessful housing rehabilitation programs that followed the riot. The government backed millions of dollars in rehabilitation loans for developers, who then sold shoddily restored houses, usually at inflated prices. Many of the houses were sold to buyers who were financially unable to maintain them. There were frequent defaults and abandonments. In virtually every neighborhood there are rows of boarded-up homes, between 35,000 and 50,000 of them throughout the city. Even many of the existing homes are substandard, small, poorly built to begin with, badly maintained.

Few developers are willing to assume the risk of building, and landlords despair of making repairs. The poverty-stricken are so short of funds that it is not unusual to find as many as ten people living in a single room. In such crowded conditions, people are quick to take to the streets, looking for mischief. They are quick to exhibit murderous frustrations brought on by crowded conditions.

The most conservative estimate is that it would take $5 billion to rebuild the core of the city. Washington is unlikely to produce that amount of aid, and the automobile industry, the richest and largest employer in Detroit, has historically taken more from the city than it contributes.

Police Officer Joe Novack, taking a coffee break during his shift, sighs and says that what he fears most are the summer months—"the long, hot summer. They're restless out there, jumpy, unhappy, doped up, and everybody has a gun. This is a city walking on eggs, and I wouldn't be surprised if we had another riot."

"There is widespread agreement that the most disturbing situation here is the city's school system," says Reginald Stuart, the chief of the New York *Times* Detroit bureau.

The schools have 236,000 students, 80 per cent of whom are black. The system is troubled by crime, dropouts, and the will of the voters, who have refused to approve an increase in the school tax rate since 1966. About 10,000 public-school students in grades nine through twelve drop out each year. Even to those who remain in school, the system delivers what is generally regarded as a second-rate education, because there isn't enough money to pay for first-class teachers and facilities.

The Police Department has a special squad that does nothing but try to keep peace in the schools. It patrols school grounds at night with dogs, looking for arsonists and muggers. By day, sex offenses, extortion, assaults on teachers, and narcotics use are common. At one school, in 1977, a man walked into a classroom and, in front of twenty-five second-graders, pumped five shots into the head of the teacher, who was his estranged wife.

Summing up the atmosphere in Detroit, Herbert Hill, labor director for the NAACP, says: "The condition of black people is already more desperate than it was during the riot in 1967. As in the past, social and economic forces will generate a ghetto rebellion that may require us to regard that disorder as a mere prelude."

Perhaps the best thing to emerge from the insurrection in 1967 was the formation of the God Squad. Although the God Squad wasn't organized until six years after the riot (a period in which conditions had not noticeably improved for blacks), one of the stated aims of Bill Paris and the handful of other ministers who founded the Chaplain Corps was to make sure there would never be another riot. It was that argument that finally persuaded the police to allow the formation of the God Squad.

The God Squad has become the cutting edge of reform, tolerance, goodwill, and understanding in Detroit. Even though their number is comparatively small, the thirty-nine members of the Squad are ubiquitous. And there are those in Detroit, police officials among them, who maintain that, without the God Squad, the city might have experienced another riot. At the very least, the God Squad has helped keep the lid on.

CHAPTER 5

Siege at St. Leo's

The man who rang the bell at Father John Morel's church door was well-dressed, polite, young, and black. It was almost eight o'clock on a sweltering, charbroiled, August night in 1977.

"Do you know where I can find a job?" the stranger asked Father Morel, who had joined the God Squad "the first day it started" in 1973.

"No, I'm sorry, I don't," the priest said as he welcomed the man into a small anteroom near the rectory. "A lot of my own parishioners are out of work too. But why don't you try the Department of Human Resources in the morning?"

The man asked if Father Morel would look up the address of the government employment agency in the phone book.

Father Morel turned his back on his visitor, walked to a small table and began leafing through the yellow directory.

Then he heard his visitor say in a soft but firm voice: "Turn around slowly. I've got a gun in my hand and I want your money."

The visit from the stranger had taken on a new, frightening dimension. Father Morel, a silver-haired, energetic, sixty-four-year-old priest with sky-blue eyes, wheeled slowly and faced the intruder, who had a brown paper bag over his hand.

Father Morel's first thought was that the man was bluffing, there was no gun under the paper bag. But he couldn't be sure. In the dim light, the man's eyes shone intensely. It was a moment of confrontation, not for preaching. Was there a finger coiled against a trigger? Was there even a trigger? Only a few months before, a priest was killed by a gunman at a nearby church. Nobody really knew what had happened, and the murderer hadn't been caught. There were no witnesses. A nun had found the priest several hours after he'd been shot to death. The priest's wallet was gone.

Father Morel removed all the currency he had from his pocket—three dollars—and handed it to the holdup man.

Hearing voices in the rectory, the robber ordered Father Morel inside. A meeting of the church's Christian Education Committee was in progress.

"I think this fellow wants your money," Father Morel announced to the eight men and women present.

There was a hassock in the middle of the room, and the holdup man ordered his victims to place their wallets and purses on it.

The loot came to about forty dollars plus some change.

The thief then ordered the men in the room to lie down on the floor.

"Better do as he says," Father Morel said. The man still hadn't shown a gun, but the memory of the other Catholic priest who'd been killed kept running through Father Morel's mind. Maybe this man was homicidal too.

As the men lay prone on the floor and the lone female victim cowered in a corner, obviously frightened, the intruder swept a small portable television set off a side table, wrapping the cord around his free hand. There was no other apparent loot in sight and the man started to leave. Suddenly he asked, "Who owns that blue Chevy outside?"

One of the men on the floor acknowledged ownership.

"Give me the keys," the robber demanded.

"I've only had the car a few months. It's practically brand-new," the man said. "I saved three years to buy it. Couldn't you forget about the car?"

"The keys, or I'll blow your head off."

The keys were passed over and the thief said as he departed, "I want all of you to stay the way you are for ten minutes."

As soon as they heard the motor of the Chevy catch and race off, Father Morel called the police.

The stolen Chevy was found abandoned five days later. The robber was never caught.

If anything, Father Morel is a resilient man. Born in Brussels, Belgium, he's been in Detroit since 1955. The fact that not even Detroit churches manned by God Squad members are safe from crime doesn't surprise him. Crime at St. Leo's is as much a part of the atmosphere as the Bible.

Everything that isn't nailed to the ground has been stolen from the church: radios, television sets, electrical appliances, car batteries. "I have a pickup truck, and the spare tire is well hidden under the trunk," says Father Morel. "But even the spare tire was stolen. I've had three bicycles stolen. So I don't buy any more bicycles. Onetime, someone stole a spare amplifier and a tape recorder during Mass."

St. Leo's faces Grand River Avenue, which was one of the areas hardest hit during the 1967 riot. It is one of the city's oldest churches, founded in 1889. The venerable building is surrounded by boarded-up stores and houses. The neighborhood is in decay.

The parish was in its heyday in the twenties, when the city was booming. It was a vital part of the neighborhood's life, with more than a thousand white parishioners. There was a grade school and a high school and a huge convent. Membership was so large that two Masses were conducted on Sundays simultaneously—one in the basement, which is as large as the church itself, and one upstairs.

Whites began trickling out of the neighborhood after World War II. But the real exodus began after the 1967 riot, when practically all the white people who could afford to moved away. Membership in the church is down to two hundred worshipers, 85 per cent of them black.

"In terms of membership and financial support, the black people haven't made up the gap," says Father Morel, spreading his hands in a gesture of helplessness. "St. Leo's is like a huge white elephant."

When Father Morel came to St. Leo's there were four priests and two dozen nuns. Now he is the only priest left. Five of the nuns remain. The high school has closed, and the grade school has moved into the high-school building. Father Morel lives in the tiny house the church once provided for the janitor.

Though he is besieged and beleaguered, Father Morel doesn't think St. Leo's should be closed. "Other churches in Detroit have it much worse," he says.

There have been several cases where entire congregations have been held up at gunpoint just at the moment the collections were completed and brought to the altars. Heist men even rob people at funeral parlors. People in sorrow sitting and viewing the corpse are ordered by two-man robbery teams to empty their wallets and purses.

Though he is nearing retirement age, Father Morel would not prefer a more comfortable assignment in a safe suburban parish.

"In the first place, my conscience would bother me. Secondly, I would get in trouble with such people, because I would tell them to do more for the poor."

Father Morel isn't a social or political radical. "But I think we are like an ostrich who puts its head in the sand and figures there's no danger," he says. "That's what we've done with our cities. Instead of people facing the problems, they have moved away from the problems. But now, with the rise in suburban crime and more integration of neighborhoods, they are being forced to face the problems anyway. And there's no place left to run.

"There's no more American Dream," he adds sadly, "and there won't be an American Dream again until we revitalize our cities."

To underscore the point, Father Morel says that the soup kitchen, that dreaded necessity of Depression America, has returned to Detroit. Daily, Father Morel provides a soup kitchen at St. Leo's.

"You see such a troubled parade of people pass by," he says. "Teen-age prostitutes and dope addicts. Men in their twenties to thirty-five and forty without jobs. But mostly old men without work or families."

One day in 1977 a dead body was found under a pew in St. Leo's. Father Morel knew the man. He was a sixty-year-old who'd had a history of heart trouble. He was at the soup kitchen every day.

"He wasn't very pleasant to smell, because he apparently had been dead a couple of days, and it was summertime, and, of course, blood was running out of his mouth and nose and flies were swarming all around."

The coroner said the man died of a heart attack. When Father Morel preached at his funeral, no one came to mourn the man.

Father Morel's face brightens when he talks of the God Squad. "It may be the only hope we have."

One of the underlying motives in starting the Chaplain Corps, he recalls, was the 1967 riot. "We all had that in the back of our minds. If we could, we wanted to use the Corps to prevent another riot."

In Father Morel's view, one reason for the riot was a deep-seated estrangement between the police and the people. That became apparent during the outbreak. The resentment was mutual. The police resented the people and the people resented the police.

"To a large extent, the community still distrusts the police and the police distrust the community. The community looks at the police as an occupation army, and the police look down on the people as good-for-nothing.

"That's another very important reason for the existence of the Corps. We try to build a feeling of trust between both sides, we try to bridge the gap."

Soon after he joined the Corps, Father Morel recalls, a number of policemen were murderd—"about a dozen in a short period of time."

He went to the funerals of all the slain officers. "That's where I got to know the other chaplains in the Corps. All the members of the city council and the police brass were also at the funerals, and I got to know them too. It's a shame to say it, but it became like a family reunion."

Father Morel was one of several chaplains called out on God Squad duty when school busing began in Detroit in 1976.

"The whole city was on pins and needles. Nobody knew how it was going to turn out," he says. "It could have been like Boston or a lot of cities in the South.

"I made the rounds of a number of schools in the 2nd Precinct with an inspector, and fortunately everything was pretty normal.

There was some tension, a few fistfights I helped break up, but I would say Detroit's busing program was very calm and orderly. It went as well as anywhere in the country—better, in fact, than in many places."

Father Morel says he's not as active in the Corps as he'd like to be. The main reason is that he's needed on home ground, to guard his own church.

Nothing has been quite the same for Father Morel and St. Leo's since the night he and his parishioners were held up. He's installed heavy wire screens on every window of every building in the church, a burglar-alarm system, and an electric eye.

"I also have dogs, a German shepherd and a collie. I was afraid that people would resent the dogs, but they don't. They figure it is a part of the urban scenery."

Father Morel usually retires about 10 P.M. Before he goes to sleep, he checks the screens, activates the burglar alarm and the electric eye, and sets the dogs loose on the grounds.

"The dogs bark every night, and they wake me up," says the priest, who is more a prisoner than a free man in his own church. "There are all kinds of strange noises at night. Sometimes it's only a car door slamming or somebody hollering. Sometimes you hear an explosion."

Father Morel's fear of more break-ins, of another gunman, is real, and the thought is never out of his mind for long.

"There is no real protection, not even for a church," he says with resignation. "Every time you open the church door, you take your life in your hands. But I have an obligation and responsibility to open the door.

"If you're not willing to live with that, then you had better pack your bags and go someplace else."

Father Morel doesn't plan to ask for a transfer. "Even though I wouldn't want another assignment, I'm interested in surviving. I'm very interested in protecting my own life."

Therefore, Father John Morel, a lifelong priest dedicated to the service of the Prince of Peace, has bought a gun. He sleeps with it under his pillow every night.

CHAPTER 6

The Quiet Passion of Peter Thomsen

Even though her husband has been a member of the Chaplain Corps for five years, Mrs. Peter Thomsen's stomach churns with fear and dread every time a call comes for him to take part in any God Squad activity.

Now, as the phone rang in the immaculate kitchen of the small home adjoining St. Peter's Danish Lutheran Church, she sensed there was peril. She always knew when there would be a God Squad call and when it would be a particularly dangerous assignment. Mrs. Thomsen had seen Rose Paris a week ago, and saw that Rose was still drowning in grief for her husband. Mrs. Thomsen was fearfully afraid of becoming a widow too.

The call *was* from the God Squad's liaison officer, Ed McQueen. Mrs. Thomsen, who'd answered the ring, passed the instrument to her husband as if it were a live snake.

Chaplain Thomsen left his dinner and took the call. Fifty-six years old, with the shoulders of a football lineman, he is a mild-mannered minister, with cerulean-blue eyes and dark-framed eyeglasses.

"There's a barricaded gunman in a drugstore near where you live," Sergeant McQueen said. "Can you get to East Monroe right away?"

Leaving his dinner unfinished, Chaplain Thomsen took a few minutes to don his official God Squad uniform—clerical collar, blue jacket, gray shirt and trousers. Squad members had adopted the uniform to distinguish them from the police, which sometimes is a critical factor in dealing with people engaged in a lawless act.

On the ten-minute drive to the scene, Chaplain Thomsen smiled inwardly. He had read an item in the evening paper which reported that police chaplains in New York City were earning $25,000 a year and asking for a $5,000 annual increase. Chaplain Thomsen and his wife made do on $650 a month. His God Squad work was unpaid—he wasn't even reimbursed for gasoline—and New York City chaplains, so far as he knew, never were called into the field to face down a man with a gun.

A different drummer motivated Chaplain Thomsen's work in the God Squad, which he had joined "the moment it was invented."

Chaplain Thomsen drew his strength for his participation in the work of the Corps from Matthew 25:36: "I was in prison, and ye came unto me." That's what the God Squad was all about, answering the cries of those who were prisoners of drugs, alcohol, depression, anger, frustration, poverty—the sad and savage litany of people whose burdens could be lifted if they had Christ in their lives.

State and local police had already flooded the small shopping mall where the gunman was holed up. An ambulance was waiting. So was a quickly gathered crowd of more than a hundred onlookers, who were being held back by uniformed officers.

Parking his car behind the ambulance, Chaplain Thomsen walked to the inspector in charge and introduced himself.

"Glad you're here," the inspector said. "Stick around."

"If you need me in any way, I'm available."

"It's a very tough situation. He's got three hostages in there. Two people who got out told us what happened. He's just a kid, tried to hold the place up. The manager tripped the alarm and the kid panicked. Instead of running, he took the manager and two women customers hostage. He's got a gun."

"Do you have a telephone line into the store?"

"Yeah," the inspector said. "We've been talking to him for more than an hour. It really bothers me because he doesn't sound scared. It's going to be a bloody night."

"Let me talk to him," Chaplain Thomsen said.

"You can try."

The open line into the drugstore was connected to a public phone in the mall.

"I'm a police chaplain," Peter Thomsen said evenly.

"So what!" was the gruff reply.

"How old are you, son?"

"Eighteen."

"What's your name?"

"Why do you want to know that?"

"If you give me your name and a phone number I can have your wife or mother or father come over here and talk to you."

"I ain't married. And I don't want to talk to my folks."

"Son, do you believe in God?"

A pause. Then: "Yes."

"If you really do believe in God, do you know what He would want you to do?"

"Yeah. Throw away my gun, give up, and go to the joint for fifty years."

"No. I'm not asking you to throw away your gun."

"Then, why are you talking to me?"

"Because I think God wants me to come in there and exchange myself for one of your hostages."

"No deal. You're a cop, and I don't like cops."

"I work with the police, but I'm not a cop."

"Same thing."

"You have two women in there. Let the older one out and I'll replace her. I don't have a gun. I'm not not trying any tricks. I just want to come in and talk to you."

"No!" The gunman slammed the phone down.

Doggedly, Chaplain Thomsen kept calling back. On and off he talked with the gunman for five hours, learning that his name was Roger Corbett, that he was a high-school dropout, had sung in a Baptist choir as a child, and couldn't find a job.

Finally, Corbett said: "I'm on H and I'm getting to the place where I need a fix."

"I'll see that you get whatever you need," Chaplain Thomsen answered.

"Then, you come in, but no funny stuff; otherwise, I'll kill these people."

Chaplain Thomsen began the longest walk of his life. After getting the okay from the inspector to enter the drugstore, he began the fifty-yard walk from the phone booth to meet Roger Corbett.

The chaplain, exhaling deeply, put his hand on the doorknob. He realized that in seconds he would be in a situation similar to that which led to the death of Bill Paris at the Addison Hotel. Nevertheless, Chaplain Thomsen pushed the door open.

The chaplain never got the opportunity to meet Roger Corbett. As the chaplain entered the store, his eyes locked with Corbett's for an instant. Then Corbett turned the gun on himself and pulled the trigger.

By the time a doctor reached Corbett's body, he was dead. The three hostages were treated for shock and released. That night, Chaplain Thomsen phoned Corbett's parents. He told the slain man's sobbing mother that he was sorry he couldn't have helped more. Three days later, Chaplain Thomsen attended Roger Corbett's funeral.

If Corbett had agreed to the exchange of hostages, Chaplain Thomsen had no specific plan for dealing with him.

"I would just have to let it happen," Chaplain Thomsen said afterward. "I am not naïve, and I don't claim to have the skills of a psychiatrist. I wasn't there to play make-believe. I made the offer to trade myself for one of the hostages without any illusions about any ability of my own to talk that man out of doing whatever he was going to do.

"Don't think I wasn't scared. All I can say is that this was one of those moments in life when you take a risk of laying down your own life if you have to. It isn't anything you intellectualize about at the time. All you know is that there are three helpless people in there. If you can get one of them out by going in yourself, you do it, that's all. You make whatever bargain you can make.

"The courage, if you want to call it that, comes from my Christian faith. What greater gift can a man give than his own life for another? It sounds kind of noble, but it isn't. Christ, in my position, would have done the same thing. To be really human and to function in the image of God means to be a person not just for yourself but for others. That, to me, is the whole story of the Bible. It is what Christ is all about.

"I felt sorry for the young man. Such a waste of a young life. But I was relieved," Reverend Thomsen says. "I am as human as anyone else. I didn't want to lose my life any more than you want to lose yours. I am at an age where I want to keep my life. My life is precious to me. I wasn't there to try and play the hero, and I hope I never get another call like it. It scared my wife terribly. She never likes it when I get a call from the Police Department. She'd like me to get out of the Corps, because she worries. I understand now why a lot of policemen's wives worry."

Chaplain Thomsen pastors a ninety-five-year-old church for Danish immigrants and their children.

"There is a question as to how long we can continue," he says ruefully. The church has 310 families on the rolls, but only 150 are active. White flight, assimilation, and "a loss of that need for a definite Danish identity" are all contributing factors to the decline of the church.

"Recent Danish immigrants," Chaplain Thomsen adds, "are not very church-minded. They integrate rapidly, and if they are interested in a church they join a denomination in their own suburban neighborhood rather than travel ten to twenty miles to St. Peter's.

"But the problem is more than the survival of my church. Actually, I view the entire city as my church," Chaplain Thomsen says with conviction. "That's why I joined the Corps, because the city needed and continues to need the Corps. To put it in its simplest Christian context, the Corps is good fighting evil."

While still in training, Chaplain Thomsen took his first ride in a patrol car.

"What was your reaction?" Bill Paris asked him afterward.

"I felt terribly uncomfortable, out of place, and somewhat overawed."

Bill Paris replied: "If the police make you feel that way as a white man, how do you think black people feel?"

The training also taught him, says Chaplain Thomsen, "that most of us don't understand the policeman's job. He is the only figure in the entire legal system that is always visible, whether he is riding in his car or walking a beat. He's out there wearing the uniform of authority, and nobody likes him. What came through very clearly in the training is that almost everything a cop does is met with resistance from somebody."

Chaplain Thomsen says he also had to cope with the suspicions of the police. As part of God Squad procedure, a chaplain, as he joins a patrol-car shift, asks the officers for their badge numbers and their car number. Each chaplain keeps a detailed log of what happens during his shift.

"I had to convince the officers that I wasn't there to spy on them. I offered to let them read my log but they remained very suspicious. I had the feeling they looked upon me as a social worker, a do-gooder who was really out there to check up on them. They seemed always on guard, never relaxed."

As a shift started, Chaplain Thomsen would tell the two officers in the car: "I'm not here to interfere with your job, but if you abuse a person verbally or in any other way I feel is unfit, I am going to call that shot as I see it and it is going to be told to the precinct commander."

In the thousands of hours he's spent with the police, the chaplain says, he's seen no instance of abuse. "Quite the contrary, they lean over backward to be fair."

In his own unobtrusive way and despite his wife's opposition, Chaplain Thomsen has become one of the most active, most committed members of the God Squad.

About a year after Roger Corbett's dramatic suicide, Chaplain Thomsen became involved in an entirely different kind of suicide case.

Again the phone was a live snake as Mrs. Thomsen handed her husband the instrument at 5:45 A.M. A high-ranking officer in the Police Department, the lieutenant on the line said, had killed himself. It appeared that he'd shot himself with his service revolver in his bathroom.

The dead officer's family must be in turmoil, Chaplain Thomsen thought, hopping out of bed. As he put on his Chaplain Corps uniform, his first reaction was that he had to reach them as soon as possible. Perhaps he could calm them down; at least his presence might comfort them. He was at the house in northwest Detroit at 6:30 A.M.

He met two homicide detectives at the front door and they went in together. A number of police officers in uniform were standing around the living room.

The widow was pointed out to Chaplain Thomsen. He went to her and introduced himself, expressing his sympathy.

"I don't want to talk to anyone now," she said quietly. "I just want to think this thing through and ask, Why, why, why did he do it?" She walked away from Chaplain Thomsen through the swinging door into the kitchen.

Chaplain Thomsen followed her into the kitchen to say: "I'm very sorry about what happened. I just want you to know that I care. I'll stay around for a while. Perhaps you'll feel like talking later."

The widow ignored him.

Chaplain Thomsen next met the dead officer's sixteen-year-old son, sitting forlornly on the living-room couch. The boy was pale, visibly shaken, and looked bewildered and in a great deal of pain. The youngster couldn't talk. He took Chaplain Thomsen's arm, held onto it, and sobbed uncontrollably.

The dead man's daughter-in-law came up to Chaplain Thomsen. Her husband, she said, was the dead officer's oldest son, who was also on the police force, working as an undercover narcotics agent.

"I'm very worried about Frank. I'm afraid of what he might do to himself when he finds out his father's dead."

At that moment Frank arrived, looking like a drug dealer fresh off the streets, wearing an old beat-up leather jacket, a rancid-smelling cap, and dirty jeans.

"Where is he?" Frank screamed.

"Upstairs," Chaplain Thomsen replied.

As Frank started up the stairs, the chaplain tried to restrain him. Chaplain Thomsen suggested that the distraught son calm down before viewing his father. The son pushed Chaplain Thomsen aside like he was a bag of feathers. He raced up the steps and was gone about five minutes. When he came down, he seemed in full control of himself.

By now, the widow had also calmed down, and the family and Chaplain Thomsen gathered in the kitchen and talked about making arrangements for the funeral.

Though he spent perhaps only two hours on that call, the memory lingers with Reverend Thomsen. For one thing, he says, why the officer killed himself was never precisely determined. There were rumors, nothing more than rumors, that the officer, who was in his fifties and had been on the force for more than twenty years, was being investigated by federal agents who suspected he was part of a drug-smuggling ring.

"If that was true, the man's suicide perhaps was understandable," Chaplain Thomsen speculates. "He couldn't stand that kind of accusation. He just couldn't bear it. But no evidence has ever come to light that he was involved in drug traffic.

"I've been told that the report on the cause of death will never be made public. Certainly, if the man was involved with drugs it would compromise him posthumously and perhaps make his son, who is still on the force, a suspect too."

Chaplain Thomsen feels there are other unanswered questions in the case, but his attempts to learn the truth from the Police Department brass have been futile.

"Either they don't know, or they don't want to talk about it. Is the Department covering up? I don't know. Theoretically, it could have been murder. For one thing, the medical examiner told me that there were no powder burns on his hand. Secondly, he shot himself in the chest—twice! I just don't understand how that's possible.

"If the Department at its very top level is honest, and I have to believe it is, I've got to feel that they're still working on the case. One day, perhaps, the truth of what really happened in that house will come out."

Chaplain Thomsen stares vacantly at his visitor and shrugs. "For the time being, only God knows the truth."

An undoubted suicide attempt was involved in another call that

Chaplain Thomsen answered a short time later. He got the call from the commander of the 16th Precinct.

"The wife of one of our officers tried to kill herself last night," the commander said. "She's at Detroit General. Can you talk to her? It's a particularly nasty case."

Half an hour later, Chaplain Thomsen was with the petite, dark-haired young woman.

"I know why you're here," he told her, "so you don't have to try to keep it from me. I am not embarrassed by what I've heard. Why don't we talk about it."

The young wife's words came out in a torrent. The cause of her suicide attempt sounded like something out of Joseph Wambaugh's novel *The Choirboys*.

"My husband wanted me to go with him to a party Saturday night," she said. "He'd been to parties like this before. I had always refused to go. But this time he talked me into it. It was a bunch of young policemen going on a hayride. It turned out to be an orgy. It was wild. There was wife-swapping and open sex. My husband got drunk and then he started flirting with other women. Everyone was doing the same thing. It was all sex and booze. It was beyond my morality, and I couldn't handle it."

She left alone, went home, and took an overdose of Nembutol. She was found in time by her husband and rushed to the hospital, where her stomach was pumped.

"Do you mind if I talk to your husband?" Chaplain Thomsen asked.

"Go ahead," she said. "If you can do us any good with his sick attitude, it will be a miracle."

The young policeman was abrupt, barely polite, as he invited Chaplain Thomsen into his house. It was one of the few neighborhoods in Detroit that was all white.

"I've been to see your wife. I know everything that happened. Maybe I can help," Chaplain Thomsen began.

"If you're here to offer counseling, I don't want it. I don't want to see a minister. I admit that I got more engrossed in the party than I should have, but you have to put that down to the pressure of my job. I was just trying to have some fun."

As they talked, it became obvious that the officer was uptight about other facets of his job. He resented the influence that black officers were gaining in the Department. In particular, he resented his commander, who was black. He didn't like taking orders from a black superior. He didn't like the idea that his black commanding officer had called in a white chaplain. Also, he didn't think much of the Department's policy of using women police officers.

There was no budging the officer from his bigotry.

After they had talked for about an hour, Chaplain Thomsen said: "What your wife did was very serious. She almost died."

"That's between my wife and me. I don't want to talk about it, and I don't want to talk to you ever again."

"If you change your mind, I'm always available. Even if you want to use me as a wastebasket, I am available. Maybe I can't help you but I can at least be a wastebasket, and that sometimes is all one person can be to another."

Chaplain Thomsen reported back to the officer's commander. But he didn't relate to the commander the officer's prejudice against blacks or why his wife had attempted suicide.

"I felt somehow that I had failed," Chaplain Thomsen said. "Still, no one can control the off-duty behavior of policemen. Certainly, they have pressures on their jobs, but that doesn't excuse open sex and orgies and drunkenness.

"A change in morality has to come from within the person himself, with the help of God. To put it in Christian terms, I proclaim the gospel, then I just let that gospel do its own work and hope that it will come to life for people in their relationships, in their work, in their attitudes. But I can't go out and do that in every case. That's got to be done by a power greater than mine."

Chaplain Thomsen learned later that the couple divorced, that the officer left the Department, and that the wife was awarded custody of their three-year-old daughter.

"All you can do is extend a helpful hand. If a person doesn't want it, as that officer didn't, you can't force him.

"I would have liked to help that couple. But if they didn't want to work through their problems with me, maybe it was better that they got a divorce. I hate to see a divorce, but I also hate to see people living together who despise each other and can't understand each other."

The story of seventeen-year-old Mary Gillette had a happier ending. An inspector telephoned Chaplain Thomsen and said he had received a call from a civilian, requesting the assistance of a chaplain. Would he handle the matter?

Chaplain Thomsen dialed the number and a woman with a well-mannered voice answered. "I don't know how to say this, but my daughter is in jail . . . on a prostitution charge. My husband and I want to get a message to her. Would you tell her that we love her?"

"Yes, but first I'd like to talk to you and your husband."

Mary's parents didn't live in Detroit, but in a newer suburb, Dearborn Heights. The house was expensive and the couple were obviously affluent. Mary's father said he owned a chain of furniture stores.

"I want Mary to know," her mother said, "that if she needs psychiatric help, we're prepared to provide it."

"And we'll take care of the hospital bills," the father said.

Chaplain Thomsen wondered why a girl would leave a well-appointed home with loving, concerned parents for a life of prostitution on the dangerous streets of Detroit.

He went to see Mary at the Detroit city jail. When he conveyed the message from her parents, she began to cry. She confessed that she had been arrested twice before on prostitution charges.

"I have this pimp, and I can't seem to get away from him. I don't like what he makes me do, but for some reason I do it anyway." Mary said she'd run away from home a number of times because her father had a violent temper and beat her. Her father, in fact, had beaten her since she was a little girl. "We're Catholics, and I don't think God approves of a father beating his daughter. Oh, Chaplain, it's hopeless. My social worker has tried to help me, and it hasn't worked. When I get out of here I'll go home, my father will beat me again, I'll run away again and go back to my pimp."

Chaplain Thomsen called Mary's social worker, who told him: "Mary doesn't need psychiatric treatment. It's already been tried. I talked to her psychiatrist, who said she's an intelligent girl with a fairly stable personality. She is able to handle most situations. What she needs is a supportive group, a small community of her peers where she feels comfortable and yet can, to some extent, live independently. She's not going to get that from her parents."

"Is it true her father still beats her?" the chaplain asked.

"Yes, I've seen the welts."

"Then, it's also true that's the reason she keeps running away from home."

"Exactly."

Chaplain Thomsen and Mary's social worker joined forces. Together, they found a Catholic home run by nuns who provide shelter for girls with problems. Mary consented to give it a try.

Chaplain Thomsen called Mary a number of times and visited her on a few occasions.

"I'm about to reach a very important decision in my life," she said on his last visit.

After she'd been in the Catholic home for six months, Mary Gillette called Chaplain Thomsen and, with an eager lilt in her voice, told him: "Guess what? I've decided to become a nun."

When Chaplain Thomsen told his wife the news about Mary, Mrs. Thomsen was overjoyed. She was proud that her husband was able to help Mary. Nevertheless, she still cringes with fear each time the phone rings. Maybe this time, she thinks, her husband won't return from his God Squad assignment.

CHAPTER 7

Among Other Matters, a Prayer for Jenny Johnson

Chaplain Isaiah D. Patterson is an evangelist for two causes he considers holy—the Bible and the Detroit God Squad. "They're both the work of the Lord," he says.

An infectious whirlwind of a man, Chaplain Patterson, the assistant pastor of Greater Grace Temple in northwest Detroit, was born in Philadelphia fifty-five years ago. Natty in a blue suit and a polka-dot tie, he declares enthusiastically that, in contrast to most churches in Detroit, "Greater Grace is booming! We don't have enough room. People are coming from everywhere."

Ten years ago, the church was foundering, was $90,000 in debt, and had less than 200 in attendance. Today, it is perhaps the fastest-growing church in Detroit, with 1,500 members and a flourishing budget that has permitted the congregation to finance the purchase of ten buildings adjoining the temple, and an abandoned school which is being turned into a community center.

"It's amazing," Chaplain Patterson says in explaining the upsurge in his church. "We follow the pentecostal doctrine of the apostles of Jesus Christ very closely, and it seems to be working. People believe in what we're doing—speaking in tongues, baptism, and the Holy Ghost."

The church's motto is: "One Lord, One Faith, One Baptism."

"That's what people want," the churchman says. "We are gaining every day. We recently moved from a four-hundred-and-fifty-seat sanctuary to the one we have now, which holds a thousand. But we still have an overflow."

Greater Grace Temple is integrated, even though it's located in a neighborhood that is all black. "We have white people who come for the services from miles away. One white family worships with us every Sunday, and they're from Pontiac, a distance of twenty-five miles. A congregation should be integrated, because that's what Jesus taught. He invited all men to join Him in the kingdom of heaven. He didn't say heaven was only for blacks or only for whites."

Chaplain Patterson says the church draws its biblical strength from Acts 2:38: "Repent, and be baptized every one of you in the name of Jesus Christ for the remission of sins, and ye shall receive the gift of the Holy Ghost."

"People come in who say they've been short-changed elsewhere. We even have Catholics who worship with us, and it's a beautiful thing."

He joined the God Squad in 1976 after being awarded a certificate of appreciation from the city for organizing a citizen-volunteer Neighborhood Watch program, which reduced crime by 30 per cent in his corner of the tough 12th Precinct.

"We had shootings, we had serious accidents to report. We even had cases where we found police officers in trouble, and we assisted them. The Neighborhood Watch has prevented rapes and muggings, and a lot of men are in prison now who never would have been caught without our volunteers."

Chaplain Patterson still supervises the patrol, but most of his time is divided between his church duties and his fervent commitment to the Chaplain Corps.

On a God Squad run one winter night with two officers in a patrol car, the radio squawked a report of a domestic dispute. Chaplain Patterson, ten minutes later, found himself in the middle of a husband-and-wife argument, often the most dangerous type of police call. Warring marital partners may turn on the police, sometimes violently, to vent their frustrations.

Chaplain Patterson and the two police officers walked into the two-story frame house gingerly. Facing them in the living room was a forty-year-old woman holding a .22 automatic.

"I'm going to shoot him," the woman said, pointing the gun toward her husband. The husband was black, the wife white.

"You're drunk," the husband said.

Chaplain Patterson took a few cautious steps toward the woman. "Sister," he said, "let me have the gun. There's no need for a shooting."

The woman reeled slightly.

"How much have you had to drink?" the chaplain asked.

"Not enough!" she said.

"Lady, you'd better go upstairs and sleep it off," the chaplain said. "Tomorrow you'll both feel better. Now, let me have the gun."

"If I give you the gun, I won't have any protection. He'll kill me. He's jealous enough to kill me, just because I had a little drink with the man next door."

"She isn't worth killing," the husband scowled.

"Yes, he will so kill me," the woman insisted. "Tomorrow morning when you hear about it, you'll know I told you so."

By now Chaplain Patterson was only two feet from the woman. He reached his hand out for the gun.

"Give it here, sister, gently," Chaplain Patterson said as he saw the woman beginning to squeeze the trigger. Luckily, the shot went wild, and the chaplain grabbed the gun from her hands.

"No, there were no charges filed and her husband didn't kill her," says Chaplain Patterson. "I'm sure he didn't kill her, although I didn't follow the case. Sometimes a chaplain follows up, sometimes he doesn't. Often the main thing is to deal with the matter at hand, defuse the immediate situation. That's all that was necessary in this case."

Chaplain Patterson grins winningly and says: "Everyone in our church knows I'm a police chaplain, and when you have fifteen hundred people in the congregation, every fifth thing that happens in the city, somebody in our church knows about it or is involved in it."

One morning about 10 A.M., he received an anxious call from a parishioner who said her son was in the hospital. He'd been shot by a police officer. "They won't let me or his wife see him. Can you go down to the hospital and find out what's going on?"

At the hospital, Chaplain Patterson showed the officer on duty outside Lester Wilson's room his God Squad badge. He was greeted cordially and admitted immediately.

Wilson's head and half his face was bandaged. "They tell me I may lose an eye," he said.

"What happened?"

Wilson said that last night, he, his wife, and two small children had been driving on Wyoming and Puritan. His wife was at the wheel and she accidentally bumped the car in front. The driver of the car got out and started toward them.

"He was bellowing and cursing. I thought he might harm us, so I grabbed my pistol from under the front seat and got out too. When he reached our car, I told him to get back or I'd blow his brains out."

The other driver retreated about ten yards, then suddenly wheeled and fired his gun. Chaplain Patterson later found out it was a 315 Magnum "with enough force to blow a small army away." He also discovered later that the other driver was an off-duty detective.

Fortunately, the shot didn't hit Wilson directly. It exploded against the door of his car, and shards of metal had penetrated his scalp close to his right eye.

"You're a lucky man. You could be dead by now," Chaplain Patterson said.

Wilson said he had one request—before going into surgery he'd like to see his parents and his wife.

Because Wilson was under arrest on a charge of carrying an unlicensed concealed weapon and threatening an officer, which are felonies, the police hadn't allowed him any visitors. Chaplain Patterson called the precinct commander and managed to have the restriction waived.

Then the chaplain went to see the gun-wielding detective, who gave him a different version of what had occurred. He claimed he had identified himself as a police officer, but Wilson had threatened him with a gun anyway.

"There were two small children in that car. Did you think of that before you fired?" Chaplain Patterson asked.

The detective avoided the chaplain's gaze. "Wilson should have thought of that when he pulled his gun."

When Wilson's wife arrived for her visit, she turned her anger against the officer on duty at her husband's door, chewing him out in a shower of obscenities.

"Lady," Chaplain Patterson said, "this officer had nothing to do with the case. He's only here to guard your husband. Why take it out on him?"

She quieted down in a few minutes and went in to see her husband. "It's a good thing I was there to play the peacemaker," Chaplain Patterson says.

Wilson's surgery lasted four taut hours. Chaplain Patterson remained with his wife and parents in the waiting room, comforting them, asking them to trust God's mercy. Finally, a doctor emerged and told Mrs. Wilson: "Everything's all right. The surgery was successful. Your husband isn't going to lose his eye."

Answered prayers, thought Chaplain Patterson.

Three months after the incident, with Lester Wilson fully recovered and back at his job as a truck driver, the Wilsons sued the city for $1 million. Their complaint amounted to police brutality and the use of unnecessary force.

The judge threw the case out of court.

"My job in this instance was minimal," says Chaplain Patterson. "The wife was about to have a fit because she couldn't see her husband. The parents too. As a chaplain, I was able to arrange that easily. I was also able to help convince the police to drop the charges against Wilson."

What does Chaplain Patterson think of the disposition of the case?

"There was right and wrong on both sides. The detective overreacted, he was too quick to shoot at a car with small children in it. But Wilson shouldn't have had a gun in the first place. That's what triggered the whole thing."

Since the day he met Lester Wilson, Chaplain Patterson had been attempting to lead him to the Lord. Finally, after six months of effort, Wilson accepted Christ. The first thing he did after he was baptized was to get rid of his gun.

"This case," says Reverend Patterson, "is a perfect instance of how a chaplain in the Corps serves as a link between the police, the people, and God."

Chaplain Patterson also became involved in the case of Roy Browne via a parishioner who called him and said his son had been missing for two days. The worried parishioner said his son had finally gotten in touch with him—from jail, where he was being held on a charge of robbery.

Chaplain Patterson went to the jail and met Roy Browne, who said, yes, he had confessed to the robbery. However, there were extenuating circumstances.

Roy told the chaplain that he worked at a cut-rate jewelry store. He had gone to work two days ago and found that the store had been robbed. There was no sign of forced entry. Someone had apparently used a key to gain entrance. His employer accused Roy of committing the crime, which he denied.

Roy's employer, a strapping man who weighed 260 pounds, overpowered him and tied him to a chair. Then he beat Roy with a clothesline, so unmercifully that Roy confessed.

"I would have confessed to anything just to stop the beating," Roy said. He removed his shirt and showed Chaplain Patterson the welts.

The Chaplain went to the detective in charge of the case and said: "I doubt very much that Roy Browne is a thief. And why was he held two days before being allowed to get in touch with his parents?"

"Chaplain, I'm sorry, but my case load is so huge I just haven't gotten around to investigating this one."

At Chaplain Patterson's insistence, they went to Roy Browne's apartment to search for the missing jewelry. They found nothing. Next, they visited Roy's employer, who denied forcing the confession from Roy.

"I'm out one thousand dollars in merchandise," he said. "Except for me, nobody else but Roy has a key. Who else could have done it?"

Chaplain Patterson didn't know who might have stolen the jewelry, but he remained convinced it hadn't been Roy. He believed Roy's story that the confession had been whipped out of him.

At Chaplain Patterson's insistence, the charge against Roy was dropped.

"I was fortunate," the chaplain says, "in that I was able to help prove the boy innocent. And my hunch was right. Two days after Roy was released, the owner of the store called the police and sheepishly admitted that his wife had taken the jewelry. They'd been having an argument, and this was her way of getting revenge."

Another member of Chaplain Patterson's congregation called one night at 11:15 to say her father was out in the street somewhere with a rifle. "He's had too much to drink, and before he left the apartment he shot the place up. Help me find him, please help me find him," she pleaded.

Chaplain Patterson raced to the address and put the sixteen-year-old girl into his car.

They cruised the streets for more than two hours, combing the area in a vain hunt.

"Here I am riding around looking for a man I don't know and who doesn't know me," Chaplain Patterson recalled. "What's more, he's got a gun and is under the influence of alcohol. It was tense, I tell you. Here you have a situation of a man with a rifle roaming the streets who might shoot somebody, anybody. If we found him, maybe he'd shoot me."

Chaplain Patterson finally suggested to the girl that they drive to the police station and ask for aid in locating her father. She reluctantly agreed that was the only thing left to do.

To their astonishment, as they walked into the station house, the girl's father was sitting in a chair near the sergeant's desk, cowed and harmless.

The sergeant said: "He walked in here a few minutes ago, gave us his rifle, and said he had killed several people. We're checking it out."

Chaplain Patterson told the sergeant he was certain the man hadn't killed anyone. "He's drunk, that's all." Still, the sergeant had to be sure. They waited three hours until all the patrol cars in the 12th Precinct reported in. No, there hadn't been an unexplained shooting anywhere in the precinct.

Chaplain Patterson drove the father and daughter home. "It could have been a very, very different story if the police had spotted him first with that rifle in his hand." The chaplain shudders. "I think the man probably would have been shot on sight."

Driving alone one night in his car, Chaplain Patterson, listening to his police radio, heard a report that an officer had been shot. Immediately, he headed for the hospital, flashed his badge, and was admitted to the wounded officer's room.

The officer said he had been off duty and sitting in a bar when two men began an argument about a hockey game being shown on television. One thing led to another, and before he realized what was happening, one of the men pulled out a gun and started shooting. A stray bullet had wounded the officer.

"I'm tired of being shot and cut," the officer continued. "I even get shot when I'm not on duty. I try to be a good policeman, but all I get for doing my job is one injury after another." The officer threw back the blanket and showed Chaplain Patterson six bullet and knife scars on his body.

"I'm just tired, tired of it all," the officer said. "That's why I drink." He said his drinking was so bad that he was a borderline alcoholic. He'd been warned by his commander that if he was found drunk again, it would mean dismissal from the force.

"Why not stop drinking, then," Chaplain Patterson suggested.

"I can't. I just can't. The mere job of being a policeman makes me drink. You'd be surprised how many cops drink too much. When you're out there on the street, you don't know what you're facing from minute to minute. You don't know if you're going to make it through your shift. What you're facing all the time is death. I don't say it's right for me to drink because of that, but it's understandable."

"If you'd trust God instead of the bottle, you'd gain strength. You wouldn't have to resort to drinking," the chaplain said. "The very thing you're talking about, the danger you face all the time, is reason enough to stop drinking. When you're out there, you need all your faculties." The chaplain paused, then added: "There *is* a way for you to stop drinking."

"How?"

"If you believe in the Lord, He can help you. He can not only make you stop drinking, He can give you rest, He can give you peace."

When the officer was released from the hospital, he went to Greater Grace Temple and was baptized by Chaplain Patterson.

"He didn't receive the Holy Ghost that Sunday morning," says Chaplain Patterson. "But it came to him the next night while he was on patrol-car duty. The Holy Ghost just fell on him while he was in the car. He was filled with such joy that he ended up bringing his partner to the church, and he was saved too."

Chaplain Patterson says his church now numbers in its congregation seventeen police officers who've accepted Christ.

"And we use them to lead others to the Lord. One night, I was giving a Bible class lesson and I said to a couple of police officers who were there: 'Wouldn't it be beautiful if you men on the force would tell your prisoners about the Lord.'"

The next day, one officer came in with a junkie who was out on bail. He quickly gave himself to God. "We baptized him right then and there," says Chaplain Patterson. "I was a character witness at his trial, and the judge put him on probation. That man hasn't used drugs in more than two years, after a six-year habit. He's one of the finest Christians in this city."

Thanks to the police-officer members of the church, twenty-five former criminals have been led to the Lord. "Not one of them has been in trouble again," says Chaplain Patterson.

What these officers are doing, the chaplain points out, is living the Bible, putting into action the faith expressed in Isaiah 1:18:

"Come now, and let us reason together, saith the Lord: though your sins be as scarlet, they shall be as white as snow; though they be red like crimson, they shall be as wool."

The officers can look at the men they arrest and say: All right, we know you've done wrong. But we all have. You can change. God can help you change.

"See, that's the key," says Chaplain Patterson. "Not telling a person how bad he is. He already knows that. What you must tell him is that even though he's bad, he can be better tomorrow. The key is in not condemning the person in his present state of sin."

Chaplain Patterson not only believes in the miracles of the Bible, but he knows that a miracle can occur in contemporary Detroit. He knows, because he witnessed a miracle.

The girl's name was Jenny Johnson and she was nineteen years old. The chaplain and the two officers who arrived at her apartment during God Squad patrol found her in a pool of blood.

Chaplain Patterson rode with her to the hospital in the ambulance. The doctor said: "She's been shot nine times. It's incredible that she's still alive . . . but she won't be for long."

"Jenny was in surgery for eleven hours," says Chaplain Patterson. "I was there the whole time with her parents. Her father said he had warned his daughter against her boyfriend, who had a vicious temper."

An hour after shooting Jenny, the boyfriend had been picked up.

"We prayed hard," Chaplain Patterson said. "I never prayed harder in my life. I called on the Lord to see her through. I reminded the Lord of the words in James 5:16: 'The effectual fervent prayer of a righteous man availeth much.' I never doubted those words, but here was a girl with nine bullet holes in her. But I knew the Lord could save her if He chose to."

At the end of the eleven-hour ordeal, the operating surgeon told Chaplain Patterson and her parents that Jenny was going to make it, despite wounds in the legs, chest, and head.

"What more proof do you need of the power of the Holy Spirit?" Chaplain Patterson asks.

"Jenny is as good as new now.

"After her wounds healed, she came to church and accepted the Lord.

"Jenny understood the power of the Lord. I didn't have to explain it to her."

CHAPTER 8

Chaplain Carol Park

"Take off your clothes or I'll kill you!"

Barking the command to a fifteen-year-old girl named Karen was a teen-ager with a long scar rippling across his chin. Cradled in his arms was a sawed-off shotgun. His companions were four other young men and a girl. The girl was holding a German shepherd on a long leash.

The bizarre group had accosted and surrounded Karen in the brawling, gritty Cass Corridor area, Detroit's red-light district. Karen had been visiting a girlfriend and made the mistake of walking to a bus stop alone. It was shortly after midnight. There were no police cars, pedestrians, or buses in sight.

Karen was trapped, about to experience the most traumatic event of her young life. The five male teen-agers pushed her into a doorway. With no choice, Karen removed her clothing, averting her eyes from her own body. The five young males then proceeded to gang-rape her. The girl in the group giggled while the German shepherd barked ferociously. Karen's agony lasted more than an hour.

Finally discarded by the rapists, Karen dressed painfully and stumbled along the street until she reached a bar. Nearly delirious, she managed to get a bartender to call the police.

Chaplain Carol Park, the first female member of the God Squad, an intelligent, outspoken, attractive woman born in 1937, was called two days later to offer aid and comfort to Karen. The call had come from the director of a youth center who was a mutual friend of

Chaplain Park's and the violated girl. The male youth director felt that Karen should see another woman.

Chaplain Park went to Karen's west side home. The chaplain's immediate concern was to make certain that Karen had received adequate medical care and attention. "Also, to let her talk it out, cry if she wanted to."

But Karen was past crying. Nor did she want to talk. It seemed to Chaplain Park that Karen, on the one hand, was taking the experience, awful as it had been, in stride. On the other hand, she was very uptight, speaking at first only in monosyllables.

"Maybe she was afraid of me," says Chaplain Park, "or not knowing me, she felt uncomfortable. And how much of her reticence was an aftermath of the brutal rape, I don't know."

"Karen," Chaplain Park said, "I'm here to help you in any way I can."

The girl remained silent.

"Please tell me how you feel. It may help you."

"I feel all right," Karen said, adding that she'd been well-treated physically at the hospital and was no longer taking the tranquilizers the doctor had prescribed.

"I'm not sure you know," Chaplain Park said, "but I've talked to your doctor and he says you're not pregnant. At least, that's some consolation."

Karen nodded.

Under Chaplain Park's prodding, Karen began to open up a little more.

"I miss my father," she said. "My parents are divorced. I wish my mother would get married again. Better still, I wish my father would come back."

"How long has it been since you've seen your father?"

"Two years."

"Do you date boys?"

"No. My mother is very strict about that. I'm not allowed to date at all. Anyway, my mother says boys—men—are hateful."

It was apparent to Chaplain Park, solemnly so, that in these, her important, formative years Karen lacked a father figure. The fact that she didn't have a strong supportive relationship with a male, or even have a casual boyfriend, offered a significant clue to the girl's personality.

"Karen, are you religious? Do you go to church? Do you believe that there is a God who loves us all?"

"We're supposed to be Presbyterians, but I haven't been in a church since I was a little girl. I don't know anything about God."

"Tomorrow is Sunday," Chaplain Park said. "Why don't we go to church together?"

"No, I'm busy. And even if I wasn't busy, I wouldn't want to go to church."

"Is there anything else you want to talk about? Do you want to tell me about the night in Cass Corridor?"

"No, I don't want to talk about *that.*"

The visit ended inconclusively. Chaplain Park wondered why Karen hadn't cried. Why wouldn't she speak of the harrowing rape in confidence to a sympathetic listener, letting out and purging herself of feelings of guilt, anger, and shame? Why was she rejecting God? Why was she rejecting help from every possible source? It would do Karen no good to keep walking an emotional tightrope. Karen, at that point, had overcome the physical effects of the rape, but how she was handling the psychological fallout was what concerned Chaplain Park. It particularly disturbed the chaplain that Karen wouldn't even permit herself the solace and healing of God.

In the next few weeks, Chaplain Park telephoned Karen a number of times. Karen was polite but remained tightlipped. No, she said, she didn't want to see Chaplain Park again.

Chaplain Park, in a dark-blue blouse and black skirt, wearing silver earrings and a silver necklace, glances wistfully out of a ninth-floor window at the Detroit Plaza Hotel and says softly, almost in tears: "Karen committed suicide three months after the rape."

Karen, Chaplain Park adds after a long pause, had gone to an uncle, a man she liked and trusted. Karen had tried to make him a surrogate father. She wanted to bare her soul and heart to him. But the one man to whom she was ready to give her trust rejected her.

"That seemed to be the last straw and she killed herself," the chaplain concludes.

"It was odd, because you would have thought Karen would seek out a woman to talk through her problems. But she didn't know how to talk to a woman, not even her mother . . . or me. Or perhaps I didn't know how to talk to her."

Chaplain Park surmises that Karen took a fatal overdose of Seconal because of male rejection.

"The rape was male rejection in a way. Her not having a father was male rejection. And, finally, there was the rejection of her uncle. She was overwhelmed by rejection and it destroyed her."

There was one other rejection. Chaplain Park, after her visit to Karen, had sent her a Bible. It was found—unopened—among Karen's effects.

Does Chaplain Park feel that she, too, rejected Karen by not following up her case more tenaciously?

"No, not at all. I called her, I constantly offered every possible resource—myself, the church, God. Karen could have reached out for me at any time. She could have reached out for God at any time.

"In crisis counseling, you can't always go running after a person. You say you're available and let them know you're available. Maybe you don't communicate effectively, but you've got to give people the opportunity to respond to you. You can't constantly mother-hen them, be with them twenty-four hours a day, and impinge upon their dignity."

What of the gang that raped Karen?

"They've never been apprehended," Chaplain Park says. "If they're ever caught, they should be tried not for rape, but for murder."

Carol Park is a preacher's kid. Her parents met while both were serving in the Indian state of Assam. Her father was a missionary, her mother a doctor.

The Parks left India three months after Carol's birth for a new post in the Philippines. Carol was seven and a half years old when the family returned to America. She went to high school in Colorado and received a master's degree in divinity from Boston University, a Methodist-run institution (and the alma mater of Martin Luther King, Jr.). As Community Volunteer Coordinator for Project Start, a federally funded program that works to rehabilitate ex-convicts on probation who have been convicted of nonviolent crimes, she earns $14,300 a year.

Carol Park settled in Detroit eight years ago, joining the Central Methodist Church, where she is an extremely active member.

"I never really thought about becoming a minister," she says. "One has to be ordained to be a minister, but my definition of the ministry isn't limited by ordination. I had deliberately not sought ordination because of something Dr. Robert Lynn of Union Theological Seminary once said: 'Our vocation is that we are called to be Christians, and our occupation is the means by which that vocation is expressed.' So I don't think you can use ordination as the be-all and end-all for determining whether or not a person is a minister."

Carol Park joined the God Squad as a result of a conversation she had in 1975 with Reverend Ron Lund, himself a member of the Chaplain Corps.

In discussing the important work the Corps was accomplishing, Carol noted that Chaplain Lund failed to mention how it was specifically aiding women. A champion of women's rights, Carol asked: "What is the Corps doing about women victims and offenders who need help and counseling?" Suddenly, she found herself volunteering, saying it was vital that the Corps have a female member to deal with the problems of women.

"Carol," Chaplain Lund challenged, "you've got the credentials. Put your muscles where your mouth is."

Next, Carol went to Bill Paris, expressing her interest in becoming part of the Corps.

"There's no reason why we can't have a woman member. In fact, it's an excellent idea," Bill Paris said. "But we can't protect you."

"I haven't lived a protected life."

"I don't mean physical protection. Usually we can provide for that, but the language gets very salty on the streets."

"Well, I have a vocabulary too, and I know how to use it, if necessary," Carol replied, her blue eyes blazing. "Do you want a sample right now?"

Bill Paris' face broke into an ingratiating grin. "I'm sure you'll survive the training program," he said. "Welcome to the Corps."

Once she was a member of the God Squad, Carol found that "you sort of have to work out your own role. You establish your place in the Corps by the things you do and the people with whom you become involved. I've worked primarily, but not exclusively, with women."

As with the male clerics on the Squad, Carol Park had to ride with the police in patrol cars during her training period.

"That experience made me very acutely aware that our whole chaplaincy is predicated on police-community rapprochement. We are not advocates for the police, nor are we necessarily advocates for the public. We are instruments of reconciliation."

After Bill Paris was gunned down by Chauncey West, the entire Corps met to elect a new director. The mood in the room at police headquarters was understandably somber.

"It seems to me," said Chaplain Park, "that we have an obligation to Bill, and that obligation is to visit the family of the man who killed him."

No one else on the Squad had thought of that, and no one on the Squad raised an objection to Chaplain Park's suggestion. Yes, Mr. and Mrs. West should be contacted and comforted, despite the fact that their son had murdered the man they all loved so passionately. It *was* an obligation they owed Bill Paris, and it was an obligation they owed God as forgiving Christians.

Chaplain Park telephoned the West home. At first unbelieving, Mrs. West agreed to the visit. Another God Squad member, Chaplain Don Williams, accompanied Carol Park to the small frame house on the southeast side of town.

"We're not here because we bear you any ill will," Chaplain Park told Chauncey West's parents.

Chaplains Park and Williams listened while Mr. and Mrs. West recounted their son's problems, displaying a mother's and father's concern for him even though he was dead.

Mrs. West said her son had developed a drug habit while serving in Vietnam. "You send your boy out clean to be a soldier, and he comes home a dope addict. That doesn't seem right."

"We tried to help all we could," Mr. West added. "We tried to keep Chauncey in the hospital."

Says Chaplain Park: "The parents were salt-of-the-earth people. What struck me most was Mrs. West's comment that when she found out about the siege at the Addison Hotel, her son was already dead. I thought that was a tragedy—to be so abruptly cut off from her son. She'd seen him the night before when he was alive. Now, suddenly, he was gone.

"Both parents had dignity. They knew Bill Paris was a good man, and they were certainly sorry about his death, but they were grieving for their son too.

"They expressed no resentment against the police who'd killed their son. Their attitude was a sort of active resignation. I, personally, was very moved by the whole incident."

Reverend Williams concluded the visit with a prayer, which asked God for guidance, for understanding, for blessing of the West family, for support and sustenance.

Seeing the full dimension of the tragedy—the needless deaths of Bill Paris *and* Chauncey West—Carol Park cried. "By the time Don Williams ended his prayer I was in tears," she says.

Several weeks after that memorable Christian confrontation, Chaplain Park became involved in another assault case. Unlike the incident with Karen, this one had a more fortunate aftermath.

A minister in Carol Park's church called and asked if she would give succor to a middle-aged woman named Jeannie who'd been attacked by two men in downtown Detroit while she was on her way home from work.

"She was assaulted, she was not raped," Chaplain Park says. "They stripped her and injured her, but, technically under the law, they did not rape her. In the struggle Jeannie evidently dislocated an arm. As the men were about to violate her, she fainted. It freaked them out, so they left her."

Jeannie said to Chaplain Park at their first meeting: "I feel very, very dirty. I don't like myself."

"What makes you feel that way?"

Jeannie complained of physical pain as well as emotional trauma.

"Since this happened, I feel sometimes like I'm losing my mind. Also, I ache terribly, so much so that I can't sleep."

After the assault, Jeannie had been treated in the hospital for her dislocated arm. The arm felt fine. The other physical pain in her body was unexplained.

Suspecting a relationship between Jeannie's physical pain and her mental anguish, Chaplain Park asked Jeannie how long it had been since she'd had a complete physical examination.

"Years—six, seven, eight years," Jeannie said.

Chaplain Park sent Jeannie to a doctor, who discovered that she had a serious bladder problem. That was the source of her pain. The doctor began treatment at once, and Jeannie started to improve.

"Carol, I can't thank you enough for making me go to the doctor," Jeannie told the chaplain two months later when she was feeling fit. "Now I know the root of my problem was physical, that the pain was real, that it wasn't all in my mind. What a relief! Now I don't feel so bad about myself. I don't feel dirty any more."

Chaplain Park says one of her most dramatic encounters occurred one evening while she was on God Squad patrol duty in a police car. A call came in over the radio saying that a woman was being beaten by her husband.

The squad car rushed to the house in northwest Detroit. The officers and Chaplain Park found the woman with bruises and marks, including a black eye. She was hobbling about painfully.

The reason for the fight, the woman told Chaplain Park, was that her husband had accused her of seeing another man.

The officers, says Carol Park, were sort of nonplussed. They didn't quite know what to do, particularly when the woman said she didn't want to file charges against her husband.

"Well, honey," one of the officers said, "you just wait till he comes back here with a gun, and then you call us."

"Which didn't solve the problem," says Chaplain Park. "She was being left high and dry with a three-year-old son and a husband apparently capable of beating her again or killing her."

Carol Park advised the woman to take her child and spend a couple of days in a motel, until she either reconciled with her husband or decided to leave him. The woman agreed.

"The officers admitted to me that they were co-operating only because I was there," Chaplain Park said.

Two days after the beating, the woman called Chaplain Park. Sobbing, she admitted that she had been dating a man named Victor. "My husband went after Victor with a gun to kill him. But instead, he killed Victor's brother, Calvin."

The husband was in police custody. Indeed, when he arrived, gun in hand and high on drugs, he killed the wrong brother. Calvin had never laid eyes on the husband's wife. Calvin just happened to be at the wrong place at the wrong time.

The husband was sentenced to thirty years in the penitentiary. The woman divorced her husband and married Victor. Today they live in another state.

"I get a letter now and then, and apparently they're very happy," says Chaplain Park.

Early in 1977, an off-duty policeman stumbled across a holdup in progress at a restaurant. The holdup men fired at the officer, felling him.

When Chaplain Park arrived at the hospital to assist the officer's wife, she found her with two small children. She also was pregnant.

"She turned out to be a very strong and resilient person," says Chaplain Park. "Her own minister was there too. This was another instance where your primary function is being supportive. The important thing is that I was there and she had another woman to talk to."

The officer, says Chaplain Park, is still in Wayne County Hospital. "He probably won't walk again and he has yet to talk. The chances of a full recovery are not very bright."

Chaplain Park has remained in touch with the officer's wife. "She doesn't telephone me, I telephone her. She's resigned to her husband's fate. She's fortunate in that she has strong support from relatives, and the police department hasn't lost touch with her. Her baby was born, a beautiful little girl. The last time we talked she said she was looking forward to the weather breaking so she could take the baby outdoors. She said she didn't have a stroller. So we managed to find one for her."

When Chaplain Park asks about her husband, the answer is always the same. "No change," the officer's wife says.

"She has a great deal of humor," Chaplain Park observes. "I mean, what else can you do in a situation like that. You either laugh or cry."

Among other services Chaplain Park renders to the Chaplain Corps is counseling women police officers.

She cites the cases of two female officers in particular who've been on patrol-car duty for more than a year. The women told Chaplain Park they didn't like the type of people they were becoming. They said they also didn't like the fact that they were usually under tension and unfailingly short-tempered. "I'm always hot under the collar," said one, "and I take it out on my family." Both said their families agreed they hadn't been the same since joining the force.

Says Chaplain Park: "They're having difficulty adjusting to their jobs and want to know how to deal with it. Women in our society are still more protected than men. So it's a greater shock for women police officers when they encounter all this stuff in the street, the brutality, the callousness. They wonder how they can retain their humanity. They wonder how they can continue to function as decent human beings, capable of enjoying themselves when they're not on duty."

Chaplain Park suggested that the Police Department, in tandem with the God Squad, organize a special course for policewomen where ministers, psychiatrists, and other officers would speak to their problems.

The program has been initiated. "It's a very important job that needs doing," Chaplain Park says. "Policewomen are themselves being brutalized. Some of the female officers are in there to prove that they can outperform the men. They develop a four-letter-word vocabulary to prove they're as tough as the men, and they often have to work twice as hard to prove that they are physically capable of doing the job. Then they gripe because they feel the men are so lazy.

"It plays havoc with their personal lives. Divorce among them is common. If society says we're going to have women police officers, society must find a way to help them adjust to the job. I'm sorry to say that we haven't done that as yet, but in Detroit at least we're making a start."

CHAPTER 9

Rough Night in Motown

6 p.m.

Motor idling, the blue-and-white police car squats in the 2nd Precinct's parking lot, an engine of justice that will help preserve and protect a corner of the city of Detroit on this Friday night, when the action, predictably, will be at its zenith. (Even so, more than a dozen other squad cars sit idly in the parking lot—they will not be assigned to the streets tonight because of a shortage of officers.)

Inside the station house, Officers Tom Gorman and Oswald Johnson are getting their gear in readiness for their shift. Officer Gorman, a twenty-seven-year-old and a three-year veteran of the force, says he hopes tonight will be slow. Officer Johnson has been a policeman for two of his twenty-three years. He agrees with his partner: "Amen, brother, I pray for a slow night."

The God Squad representative on this shift is Chaplain William G. Reed, the sixty-six-year-old pastor of the Greater King Solomon Baptist Church. At the moment, Chaplain Reed is standing next to the sergeant's desk listening while a young man in purple slacks bellows his complaint that a friend of his has stolen his umbrella. The youth, about sixteen, is livid. "I want that fellow caught and I want my umbrella back," he demands.

"How much did you pay for your umbrella?" Chaplain Reed asks the young man.

"Three dollars. That's a three-dollar umbrella."

"Suppose I give you three dollars for another umbrella and you forget all about this."

The youth's eyes light up. The temptation to accept the chaplain's offer is there. But suddenly his chest swells with pride. "No, I want *my* umbrella."

"All right," the desk sergeant says wearily, "we'll see what we can do."

At the front door of the station house, the young man stops once more and bellows: "Be sure and call me as soon as you find the crook who stole my umbrella."

Chaplain Reed and officers Gorman and Johnson walk to their waiting car through the rear exit. It's been raining on and off most of the day. At the moment, the rain is drifting in a fine mist.

The first thing Chaplain Reed does is jostle the back seat of the police car, shining his long black plastic flashlight along the floorboard, looking for weapons and drugs secreted by prisoners snagged on the previous shift and missed by arresting officers. The chaplain has found a number of guns and knives and several caches of reds and whites in his searches.

As the car begins to roll, Chaplain Reed says the flashlight is the only "weapon" he carries when he's on God Squad patrol-car duty. The flashlight, and a verse from Matthew: "Let us go across to the other side of the lake . . . Where is your faith?"

The car is barely underway when the dispatcher, in an urgent voice, reports that a man with a rifle is barricaded in a two-story house, shooting at random into the street.

The rain begins to come down harder, and over slippery streets the patrol car, siren screaming, careens toward the location. The car is at the scene in less than ten minutes. Members of the Department's Tactical Unit, including sharpshooters, have already arrived. Other sirens hail the momentary appearance of half a dozen more police cars.

Chaplain Reed heads for Inspector Mike Long, who is in charge of what has quickly turned into a siege.

"He's been in there over an hour and luckily he hasn't killed anyone . . . yet," the inspector tells the chaplain. The remark is punctuated by a gunshot and a fierce flash of fire from the top story of the house. The chaplain and the inspector duck behind the protection of the nearest police car.

Inspector Long continues to brief Chaplain Reed: "The man's name is Roosevelt Atkins. According to his wife, he started roughing up her and their kids. She got out of there with the kids when he pulled a rifle out of the closet. She ran downstairs and called us from a neighbor's house."

"Is he on liquor or drugs?" Chaplain Reed asks.

"Neither. Just mad at the world, I guess. Exploding with anger inside."

Chaplain Reed moves his gaze 180 degrees to take in the scene. Beyond the bank of police cars, a crowd of neighbors had formed. In position, behind trees, at angles to the right and left of the gunman's eyrie, and lying flat on rooftops, are the departmental sharpshooters, marksmen who can hit a dime at five hundred yards.

"Before something drastic happens, we need somebody to go in there and try to talk Atkins out peacefully," the inspector says.

"Just what I was thinking," the Chaplain responds.

"I didn't mean you."

"I meant me."

Inspector Long tries to convince the chaplain that the situation is too risky.

"David didn't think it was too risky going up against Goliath."

The inspector shrugs and says, "You'll need a bulletproof vest."

"Never mind that," Chaplain Reed answers quietly. "My faith is stronger than a bulletproof vest. Besides, I've got God. He's enough. Anyway, if it's my time to go to heaven, then it's my time to go."

Without further fuss, Chaplain Reed leaves the protection of the police car and circles around the house, making his approach from the blind (or rear) side. The back door is unlocked and the chaplain enters, gingerly making his way up the stairs.

In a loud voice he shouts up to Atkins, identifying himself as a minister. "I'm unarmed. I want to come up and talk to you. If you'll let me, I can help you."

Roosevelt Atkins answers with a bullet. The shot carves a hole as large as a silver dollar in a wall less than two feet from where Chaplain Reed is standing.

Undaunted, Chaplain Reed keeps climbing the stairs, slowly. "There's no way out of here," he calls to Atkins. "The police are all over the place. You're surrounded."

Again Atkins' answer is the ferocious slam of a bullet, which, this time, comes closer to killing Chaplain Reed. The shot lands less than a foot from the chaplain's head.

"I'm coming in for you and you're going to give me your gun," Chaplain Reed says. "You can kill me if you want. But you'll have to explain to God why you took the blood of a man who bears you no ill will, who only wants to help you."

Chaplain Reed moves into the room with Atkins. The rifle looks like a cannon. Atkins backs up, cowering in a corner. "Don't come any closer or I'll shoot."

"What's troubling you? Tell me what's troubling you."

"I've just gone crazy," Atkins says. "I'm tired of being one of life's losers. I've been out of work more than a year. I want to shoot back at the world."

"You've got a nice family, son, and I'm sure somebody in my congregation can help you get a job. All you have to do to get out of this mess is give me your gun. Don't be too proud or too foolish to accept help."

Roosevelt Atkins collapses to the floor, dropping his rifle, as harmless now as a mound of putty.

"Are you a real minister?" Atkins sobs.

"Folks in my congregation think so. The police think so."

"Then, lead me to the Lord," says Atkins. "I need the Lord so bad. The Lord's the only thing I haven't tried. I can face anything if God is with me. At least, that's what my wife tells me."

"She's right."

Chaplain Reed puts his arms around Roosevelt Atkins, prays for him and quotes from John 3:3: "Jesus answered and said unto him, Verily, verily, I say unto thee, Except a man be born again, he cannot see the kingdom of God." He also quotes I Peter 5:5–6: "For

God resisteth the proud, and giveth grace to the humble. Humble yourselves therefore under the mighty hand of God, that he may exalt you in due time."

Arm in arm, Chaplain Reed and Roosevelt Atkins walk from the building.

An astonished Inspector Long and two sharpshooters run to meet them.

"He won't give you any more trouble, Inspector," Chaplain Reed says. "Be gentle with him. He's just found the Lord."

Subsequently, Chaplain Reed appeared in court on Roosevelt Atkins' behalf. All charges were dropped. And Chaplain Reed kept his word about finding Atkins a job—he went to work in a Ford stamping plant.

For his participation in the incident, Chaplain Reed was awarded a civilian citation for bravery by the chief of police.

"Reverend Reed's devotion to duty and courageous performance in the face of grave danger represents a response of a concerned chaplain to a community crisis," the citation reads. "Even though the gunman represented an immediate threat to his safety and to his life, Reverend Reed ignored the danger and vigorously pursued the challenge."

8:15 p.m.

Back in the patrol car, Chaplain Reed is eager to proceed to the next crisis.

The chaplain is at an age when most men have retired, but he has no intention of retiring or devoting himself to anything except the affairs of his church and his work with the God Squad. Since he joined the Squad in 1973, he's been one of its most avid, busiest members. He unfailingly rides the patrol cars every Thursday, Friday, and Saturday evenings, the busiest nights of the week for the police.

A native of Gallaway, Tennessee (population 100), he's been in Detroit for twenty-five years. He could easily pass for white. "My father was white," he explains, "and my mother was black. It's one of those things that happens when you grow up in the South."

He recalls facing a great deal of prejudice while going to school as a youngster. "I wasn't accepted by whites, and sometimes I wasn't accepted by blacks, so it was difficult. But my father, who owned property and farmed, encouraged me to stay in school and learn. I learned so much I had sense enough to become a preacher."

The patrol car, straying through southwest Detroit, receives another call. A pair of middle-aged women are engaged in a knock-down, drag-out fight on the porch of a brick home five minutes from where the car is cruising.

The officers and Chaplain Reed quickly emerge from the car and with much difficulty, amid a stream of mutually exchanged expletives, manage to separate the battling women.

The officers drag one of the women to the squad car in handcuffs. The other, still roaming free, has a whiskey bottle in her hand. The chaplain approaches her.

"Give that here," Chaplain Reed says.

She breaks off the top of the bottle, turning it into a lethal weapon.

"I'm going to cut you," she says.

Chaplain Reed shines the full beam of his flashlight into the woman's eyes. It distracts her for a moment, but she still manages to throw the bottle at the chaplain. It lands against a brick post, shattering. The whiskey and glass splinters from the bottle splash into Chaplain Reed's face.

When Chaplain Reed says his cheeks are burning from the whiskey, Officer Gorman calls for a back-up car, which arrives in five minutes. The two handcuffed women are handed over, and officers Gorman and Johnson speed Chaplain Reed to the emergency room at Detroit General Hospital.

A doctor rinses the chaplain's face, applies medication, and washes out his eyes.

"You're lucky," the doctor says. "None of the glass got into your eyes. You're as good as new."

"The woman was drunk," Chaplain Reed says on the way back to the car. "She had no idea what she was doing."

9:30 p.m.

The call this time is to a residence where a man is beating his wife. Entering the apartment, the officers move to protect the wife while Chaplain Reed walks into the kitchen where the man he confronts is holding a butcher knife.

"The best thing you can do is drop that knife—now!" Chaplain Reed says.

The man, about thirty-five and with a nasty scar on his forehead, moves closer to the chaplain, two steps closer.

"I don't know what your problem is, but anything can be settled," the chaplain says. "If you use that knife on me, you're going to be in a whole lot of trouble. Just let it go and we'll talk about whatever's bothering you."

At that moment, officers Gorman and Johnson join Chaplain Reed in the kitchen. Both officers put their hands to their guns. Officer Gorman's gun is already out of his holster.

"Hold it," says Chaplain Reed. "There'll be no need for any shooting." Chaplain Reed, calm as Christ walking the sea, goes to the man and, without resistance, removes the knife from his hand.

"We can't get along," the man says. "She's spending too much money and things just aren't right," the man explains.

"I just bought a refrigerator for a hundred and fifty dollars, secondhand," the wife says.

"What you people need is church and counseling," says Chaplain Reed. "Maybe I can show you how to live on a budget. The Lord will do the rest." The chaplain hands the husband his card and says he wants to see them both in church tomorrow morning at 10 A.M.

"I'm sorry," the man says, and goes over and kisses his wife.

10:40 p.m.

The next call is particularly ugly. The officers and Chaplain Reed arrive at an apartment where a mother has stabbed her sixteen-year-old son to death.

"I did it for him," she screams. "I did it for him. He was a junkie and he put that knife to my throat, threatening to kill me if I didn't hand over my welfare check."

In ten minutes, a contingent of police and a coroner's attendant arrive.

The woman's face is buried in Chaplain Reed's shoulder while he comforts and prays with her. Then her hands are cuffed and she's led away.

In the car again, Chaplain Reed is saying: "Most people don't realize it, but women are more violent than men. They're rough. I'll go down to the jail tomorrow and see if I can lead that poor woman to the Lord."

Officer Gorman, who is white, sees a car double-parked and obstructing traffic. He hops out and gives the black woman at the wheel a ticket. Angry, she accuses the officer of prejudice.

"You wouldn't give me that ticket if I was white," she says.

By this time, Chaplain Reed has moved into the minor fray. "You've no call to say anything like that. You are double-parked and deserve the ticket."

"He called me a nigger," the woman lies.

"No, he didn't. This is a fine officer and I heard him say no such thing."

"You're nothin' but an Uncle Tom," the woman declares.

The woman is given the ticket and the officers and Chaplain Reed return to their car.

11 p.m.

"Prejudice works two ways," says Chaplain Reed as the patrol car resumes cruising. "Sometimes a dark person will dislike me because I'm lighter. Sometimes you find blacks that thoroughly dislike whites just because they're white. I think that's the type of woman we saw in this instance. It wasn't that she got a ticket—it's just that she has a pure, un-Christian hatred for whites."

The calls from the dispatcher turn into routine. It looks as if the rest of the evening will be quiet.

Chaplain Reed sighs and scans the city streets from the rain-soaked windows of the patrol car.

"Detroit," he says, "is not a particularly religious city. In the last four years alone, I've seen my congregation decline from eight hundred members to four hundred and ten. Not only my church, but most of the others are hurting.

"At Greater King Solomon Baptist we have only about ten members who are white; but, black or white, this isn't a Christian, churchgoing city.

"People here don't flock to churches like they do elsewhere, especially in the South. It's a shame. No, it's a tragedy. We've got the only answer there is to crime in church and God. But people keep ignoring the church. They keep ignoring God."

Asked if he's ever been afraid, Chaplain Reed replies that he lost his fear as the result of a 1969 automobile accident. A huge diesel truck plowed into his Chevy head-on, totaling his car. A highway patrolman pronounced him dead, but a doctor who arrived on the scene rushed him to a hospital and managed to revive him.

It took six months for the chaplain to recover from his injuries.

"While I was lying in that hospital bed, I thought and I thought. I thanked God I was going to be all right, and I received a deeper insight into life and God.

"I had been in the ministry then about twenty-seven years, but for the first time I began to understand the nature of God. I realized that He had been protecting me in that crash. It seemed as if God was saying, 'I want to use you in my work.' That's the major reason I joined the Chaplain Corps, because I know God thinks of it as 'His work.'

"Now I have no fear of anything or anyone. Of course, I'm not foolish. I'm as careful as the next man. But fear of a gun or a knife or whatever, it's just not there. That's what comes from the wisdom of understanding God. I know that whatever happens to me is God's will."

1:30 a.m.

After a half-hour coffee break, the patrol car is heading slowly back to the station house, its shift almost over. There have been no more calls to answer this night, and it looks as if there won't be.

But suddenly the dispatcher's voice rings out . . . "Two men dead and lying on the sidewalk." The car speeds to the address.

The chaplain is shocked when he gets out of the patrol car and inspects the bodies. One of the dead men is wearing purple slacks. The youth he'd seen at the beginning of his shift complaining over the loss of an umbrella had apparently found the youngster who'd stolen it. Both had guns, and in the fight they'd killed each other.

"Imagine," says Chaplain Reed, "all this over a three-dollar umbrella!"

2 a.m.

The car wheels into the parking lot of the station house. Officers Gorman and Johnson and Chaplain Reed walk inside. The policemen hand the desk sergeant their reports.

"Pretty rough out there tonight?" the desk sergeant asks.

The officers don't answer.

"Just another night," Chaplain Reed replies, "just another night on God Squad duty."

CHAPTER 10

Fighting Pastor

"Riot!"

The word spread with hurricane force along Livernois Avenue in mid-July 1975 shortly after a white bartender shot and killed a black man who was either tampering with or attempting to burglarize a patron's car in the tavern's parking lot.

Livernois Avenue is a wide thoroughfare on the northwest side of Detroit, once known as "the used-car capital of the world." As blacks moved into the area, the car dealers moved out, leaving a lackluster commercial-residential district that quickly became a high crime area.

As word of the shooting spread, the neighborhood quickly became inflamed. A crowd of more than two thousand blacks, led by militant, no-nonsense teen-agers, swiftly formed. Brick-throwing began. Then, as the crowd moved down Livernois, fire bombs were hurled. Looting of stores and shops began almost immediately. The bar where the shooting had taken place was angrily destroyed by the crowd.

The Police Department, taken off guard, hastily mustered as much muscle as possible. In a few hours, between seven hundred and one thousand officers were on the scene. The police were in full battle regalia, including helmets and gas masks. Scores of officers carried tear-gas canisters.

Also called to the scene was God Squad Chaplain J. B. White and every other member of the Chaplain Corps who could be found. The Police Department and the God Squad feared that another full-scale disturbance was breaking out in Detroit, the worst confrontation between blacks and police since the pulverizing riot of 1967.

A police command post, including a communications center linked to headquarters, was set up outside the ruined bar. From that vantage point, Chaplain White and others in the God Squad moved into the crowd, urging them to be calm, trying to convince them to disperse, telling them to return home. Only a few took the advice.

The shooting incident at the bar had occurred about 9 P.M. on a hot summer night. By midnight, there was full-scale confrontation, although the police held back their firepower, content to keep the crowd at bay and maintain their battle line.

Besides aiding in crowd control and the soothing of emotions, Chaplain White was functioning as a one-man rumor-control center.

"It was unbelievable," he says. "There was almost a hysteria or paranoia on the part of the police officers. Most of them were white, and they felt that anything they did would be interpreted as police brutality. And, of course, they were all afraid that the momentary standoff would escalate into a riot."

The rumors sped like poison darts through the ranks of the police. Chaplain White raced from the communications setup through the lines of the police to squelch each and every rumor as soon as he heard it. The police themselves were more squeamish and frightened than the crowd.

"I hear every black in the city is headed for Livernois," one officer said. Chaplain White checked that one with headquarters and found that the rest of the city was quiet.

Other rumors he shot down among the police were that some in the crowd had gone for weapons, including machine guns, that fire bombs would be tossed into police ranks, and that the crowd would charge the police at any moment.

The standoff continued tensely for twenty-four hours. At least there had been no casualties . . . so far. The second night, the police realized the standoff couldn't continue indefinitely.

Over bullhorns, officers warned the crowd to clear the street. Sullenly, slowly, the crowd began moving north, but it did not disperse quickly enough, so the command was given to release the tear-gas canisters.

In the melee that followed, Chaplain White was hit by a flying bottle. He also inhaled some of the gas—he hadn't thought to wear a mask himself.

On a side street off Livernois, a middle-aged Polish man, who worked in a bakery as a panwasher, got in the way. A post-World War II immigrant, he had been imprisoned in a Nazi concentration camp. He had fled to America for safety. About a dozen young roughnecks pulled him from his car, beat him senseless, and killed him.

Tragic as it was, that was the only death, other than the black man who'd been slain in the tavern parking lot.

The Police Department, says Chaplain White, was fully organized by the third day. By then, the thing had wound down and petered out. He credits members of the God Squad with helping immeasurably by their visible presence and their constant injunctions to the hotheads in the mob to keep their tempers and simmer down.

"Fortunately, the crowd had no ringleader to stir them up. And the police, everything considered, used a great deal of restraint. The Police Department's show-of-strength strategy was effective."

During the entire imbroglio, the God Squad had worked tirelessly—Chaplain White had labored thirty-two hours nonstop the first night. It was a bravura performance for the God Squad, one of its finest accomplishments.

Not much justice emerged from the incident. The white bar owner went to trial, was charged with a misdemeanor and acquitted. In another trial, the gang that had killed the Polish immigrant was also acquitted.

"Perhaps the gravest test of the Detroit Police Department's capability to contain a potentially citywide disturbance was neutralized," the Department's annual report noted. "Both citizens and police share the credit for quelling the actions of a resentful crowd that gathered. . . . The crisis was geographically contained and over in three days, despite extreme provocation by certain groups.

"Not a shot was fired by a policeman during the whole incident. There were also no confirmed reports of shots fired by citizens participating in the disturbance.

"An independent survey of residents and businessmen in the area about three months after the disturbance, found more than 81 per cent rated police behavior as 'very good' or 'fairly good,' thus confirming Mayor Young's statement that the system of justice works and the community will co-operate to keep the peace.

"The price tag—$1.3 million in extra police expenses."

Strangely, the report omitted giving credit to Chaplain White and the other members of the God Squad who had done their share and more to keep the peace.

"It doesn't matter who gets the credit," says Chaplain White. "The important thing is that the riot never materialized."

The Reverend James B. White is fifty-three years old. Born in Toronto, Canada, he didn't plan to become a minister. He took his undergraduate work in chemistry at Eastern Michigan University.

"After my graduation, I was employed in chemical research for about seven years, but all my life I'd been interested in the church. I decided I wanted to serve the church as a pastor. So I changed directions. I changed from dirty water to holy water."

A neat man who wears a mustache and gold-rimmed glasses, he arrived in Detroit in 1966.

"When I became pastor of Advent Lutheran, there were six hundred or more members. Today there are only one hundred members. They are all senior citizens, all white, and all on low fixed incomes."

The church has a budget of $35,000 a year, $11,000 of which goes to Pastor White as salary. It isn't enough to support him, his wife, and two foster children. "Consequently, I am seeking part-time employment."

Emotionally and financially, Chaplain White says, "I am fighting for my life. My congregation is in jeopardy, because with only one hundred poor people on the rolls, well, what do you do in a case like that? I mean, you are really fighting for your life, for your very existence, especially when you still have the mortgage on the church to pay, and the national church doesn't have the funds to give us financial aid in order to keep us going. Yet, I think the church has an obligation to support these people in their old age."

Despite his preoccupation with a nonviable church, Pastor White volunteered to join the Chaplain Corps because "I realized there was a necessity for the Police Department to reach out further into the community and try to bring the two constantly warring factions together. That really appealed to me."

Prior to his joining the God Squad, Pastor White was the chaplain of the Detroit Police Department's Motor Traffic Section, which was responsible for patrolling the freeways. He learned how to ride an 800-pound Harley Davidson motorcycle. Duty with the traffic section was rough-and-tumble, with Chaplain White involved in high-speed chases, nerve-shattering snipings of citizens and officers, fistfights which led to gun play, vehicle rammings and tire-iron beatings. His service was cut short when the freeway crime situation became so serious that the state police were asked to assume the job.

Part of the duty of every God Squad member is to counsel members of the Police Department who are having marital or other personal problems. Repeatedly, God Squad members have remarked that there is frequently more action mediating a family dispute than riding in a patrol car.

The incidence of divorce in the Department, Chaplain White says, is abnormally high. So is the incidence of other types of family problems.

"In most cases I see, the families have hit bottom. They come to me, or I come to them, as a sort of court of last resort. Usually, they have already decided to file for divorce."

The chaplain states that policemen are basically loners. If they have any friends, they generally are other policemen. They do not mix easily with other segments of society when they are off duty, and they tend to think that their work is unique and underappreciated.

"So the distance that they create for themselves and their families is their protective device. Thus, if anyone moves in too quickly they become suspect. They wonder why a guy like me is interested in them.

"Perhaps by training, and maybe by their own basic personality pattern, they do not trust easily. This compounds the problem, because they carry this trait into their own families.

"It's not unusual for a husband who is a police officer to become suspicious of his wife and follow her. Policemen make very jealous husbands. If she has moved out of the home and into a separate residence pending a divorce, the house is put under surveillance. The phones may be tapped. That's pretty heavy stuff."

Chaplain White cites a case of seeing a policeman and his wife who had been married for twenty years. They came to him of their own volition.

"When I married him as a young woman," the wife said, "I thought he was a knight in shining armor."

Her husband, she related, had been very ambitious. In the first years of their marriage, her husband had constantly said that he was going to move up very rapidly in the Department. One day, perhaps, he would be a commander. But it never happened.

"The result is," said the wife, "that he's frustrated. Somehow he blames me for the fact that he never became more than a sergeant. But that's not my fault."

The wife, in order to relieve the boredom of her life, had sought employment. She became a clerk in an insurance company and rose rapidly to become office manager. She was now earning more money than her husband and had a position that commanded respect. Jealousy and rivalry had developed between them, leading to constant arguments. The husband wanted his wife to quit her job and tried to reassert his old dominance over her. But she wasn't having it any longer.

"I've discovered that I have capabilities too," she said firmly.

There were three children involved—a son who was a junior in high school, a daughter who was fourteen, and a younger boy still in elementary school. Chaplain White asked the couple if they could bring their children to the next counseling session. They agreed.

"It was a very wet occasion when the talk got around to divorce," the chaplain says. "All the children were crying, and that was an eye-opener for the parents. They saw the problem their bickering had caused.

"I don't prescribe peace at any price, but I thought they had to work out a solution for the children if they intended to go through with the divorce."

All of Chaplain White's attempts to reconcile the couple failed. The officer's ego had been shattered by his wife's ability to surpass him. Her ego, meantime, because of her success, was at its zenith.

She moved out of the home, taking the children with her, and the officer retired from the Police Department.

"This was a case," Chaplain White says, "in which he actually put her under surveillance. He watched her like a hawk, and he had fellow officers watching her as well. He tapped her phone. He knew about her banking affairs. It was just incredible to me."

The couple has been divorced for more than a year. But the husband's spying on his wife continues.

"I don't know if he'll ever leave that woman in peace," the chaplain says. "I don't think he fully comprehends that he is divorced, and that he's lost his family."

Another case, involving a twenty-four-year-old officer, had to be handled with unusual delicacy and discretion by Chaplain White.

One evening the young officer, after his shift, had drifted down to the Cass Corridor red-light district and attempted to pick up a prostitute. The "prostitute" turned out to be an undercover female detective.

The officer was put on trial by a police board and given a thirty-day suspension without pay. The board had also recommended counseling with Chaplain White.

"The problem was that, for this one infraction of the rules, he was going to pay a high price. He had two small children, and he hadn't yet told his wife what had happened. I didn't inform the wife either, because it would be destructive to the marriage. This is one of the cardinal rules about marriage counseling—never violate a confidence. If the officer had told his wife about it, fine. I would then have been happy to counsel both of them. But since he hadn't mentioned it, I saw no reason to bring it up."

Chaplain White arranged for the officer to have his suspension meted out two or three days at a time. "In other words, he could take a day or two off a month and pay the penalty that way. This avoided arousing the suspicions of the wife. I perhaps saved what could have been an unfortunate situation. I think the officer learned his lesson. He's still in the Department and still married."

Chaplain White, of course, takes his turn on patrol-car duty. One evening, while out on a run, the radio flashed the news that a young officer had shot himself. By the time the chaplain arrived at the hospital, the officer, twenty-two years old, was dead.

"It was a very, very sad case," the chaplain says. He talked to the officer's wife at the hospital, who told him that her husband's leg had been injured in a holdup, and ever since he'd been assigned to a desk job. But from the time he was a kid the officer had wanted to be a street cop. Brooding about his dull job, away from the action, with nothing to look forward to except life as a partial cripple, had overwhelmed him.

Chaplain White still sees the young police widow. "She's restructured her life. Of all things, she married another policeman!"

Police wives, concludes Chaplain White, are a depressed minority who carry a special burden.

"Because of the nature of their work on the force and because John Q. Public can be awfully nasty to policemen, they often take their troubles home. So it's a very difficult role that police wives have to play.

"Unless they are pretty sure of themselves, pretty sure of their marriage, they can be led into a lot of trouble. If a police officer, for example, is working on a particular assignment which may take him out of the city and he isn't home for two or three days, the wife doesn't know where her husband is. And he can't tell her. That creates a burden for the wife.

"Police wives have to be pretty stable themselves to marry policemen.

"You take the policeman's uniform away from him, take his badge away, take his gun away, put him into civilian clothes, and sometimes he is a very inadequate male. He is not the superguy he thinks he is. He is as fragile as the rest of us. More than anyone else, the policeman's wife knows that."

Of all the brave policemen Chaplain White has known, the bravest, by far, he says was Officer Brian Switzer. The officer and the chaplain met at Detroit General Hospital.

Eleven months before their meeting, Officer Switzer had participated in a narcotics raid. While breaking into the house with a contingent of uniformed and plainclothes officers, he'd been shot. A sergeant along on the raid was killed. Six people were arrested.

Chaplain White was asked by Officer Switzer's lieutenant to visit him at the hospital. The first thing the officer said, after Chaplain White introduced himself, was, "I'm going to die, I know it."

"Those decisions are made by God," said Chaplain White. "Besides, you're going into surgery again tomorrow. There's always hope."

The officer, only twenty-six years old, had been in excruciating agony since receiving his wound, despite the pain-killing drugs the doctors administered. The bullet had pierced an artery, and he'd had six operations. Infection kept recurring, and the doctors were powerless to control it.

During his entire hospital confinement, there had been a round-the-clock police guard outside Officer Switzer's room. If he recovered, he was needed to testify against the six indicted men. Threats against Officer Switzer's life had reached the Police Department: hence, the guard.

Chaplain White began visiting Officer Switzer daily, sometimes twice a day.

"At first Brian was like a lot of policemen," Chaplain White says. "He was suspicious; he wondered, Who is this guy with the collar coming to see me? He's here to give me religion."

But Chaplain White hadn't preached to Officer Switzer. "Instead," says the chaplain, "in that time I became Brian's friend."

Officer Switzer said to Chaplain White: "I'm tired of being sick. I've told the doctors to either get me well or . . . let me go."

"We'll see, Brian, we'll see," Chaplain White said. "It's still in God's hands."

During Officer Switzer's seventh operation, he was on the table for four hours. Afterward, the doctors said, guardedly, that the operation had been a success. But they were still fearful of infection. The infection did return a week later, and Officer Switzer was quickly losing his grip on life.

Chaplain White, in his visits, had kept the policeman abreast of what was happening in the outside world. Officer Switzer was a sports fan who followed the fortunes of the Detroit Tigers avidly. On days off, his greatest joy had been to take his wife Miriam with him on his motorcycle for rides in the country. Now, however, Chaplain White felt the moment had come for Brian Switzer to be practical.

"I know you're a good Baptist, so I'm not concerned with your vertical relationship to God," he said. "But I am worried about your horizontal relationship in this world."

Officer Switzer looked puzzled.

"We don't know whether you're going to live or die," Chaplain White continued. "Have you made out your will? Do you and Miriam have a joint bank account? What's going to happen to your son?"

Miriam Switzer, a dark-haired, attractive, and very worried woman, had spent every day during her husband's illness at the hospital. Her son Sean was the product of her first, unsuccessful marriage. But since she and Brian had been married two years ago, Brian had become a doting stepfather.

Officer Switzer said he didn't have a will or a joint bank account.

"If you die, everything will be tied up. I think, in all fairness to Miriam and Sean, you ought to take care of those financial details."

"You're right. I'll do it."

Chaplain White contacted the Detroit Police Officers Association. The departmental union sent an attorney to the hospital, who put Brian Switzer's estate in order.

On his last visit to his bedside, Chaplain White asked Brian if he was afraid to die.

"No, I've made peace with my maker."

The next day, Brian Switzer slipped into unconsciousness and the hands of God.

Though Brian Switzer was a Southern Baptist and Chaplain White was the pastor of Advent Lutheran Church, Miriam Switzer asked the chaplain to conduct the funeral service.

Chaplain White chose his text from Ecclesiastes 3:1–2, intoning: "To every thing there is a season, and a time to every purpose under the heaven: A time to be born, and a time to die: a time to plant, and a time to pluck up that which is planted."

In Chaplain White's estimation, Brian Switzer died a hero. "He had faced up to the reality of what had happened to him. I think he had every reason in the world to be very, very bitter about life. But he had no trace of bitterness, not even to his killer. Brian was able to ventilate his feelings to me and sort out his thoughts. That's the purpose I served. In the process, I made a brave friend I'll never forget."

Shortly after the funeral, Chaplain White called Brian Switzer's widow. "I simply told her that anytime she needed me I was there. I realized she was going through a period of grief. She needed time to mourn and she needed time to think about what she was going to do with the rest of her life."

Brian Switzer died in January 1976. Chaplain White didn't hear from his wife until almost a year later, when she sent him a Christmas card from Chicago.

"That's the only contact I've had with her since we talked on the telephone. I hope she and Sean are very busy living very happily ever after."

CHAPTER 11

Through a Glass, Darkly

On a Sunday morning in 1974, a gray-haired, feisty member of Mt. Zion Missionary Baptist church, 1,200 strong, rose from her pew to address the minister: "I heard the other day that Pastor Barlow has become involved with the Police Department. Now, that's going too far. Pastor Barlow, you may not like what I'm saying, but I'm saying it anyway. I can't find any passage in my Bible that says a minister should be running around with the police."

The parishioner had voiced a concern of many members of the church, and her complaint received shouts of agreement and much applause. It was a serious charge, and Chaplain Barlow felt he had to answer it immediately.

"It's true," he declared from the pulpit, "that I've become a member of the Chaplain Corps of the Detroit Police Department . . . and I intend to remain an active member of that organization."

He explained to his congregation that his police duty was actually a way of broadening his ministry. He emphasized the importance of the Police Department and said that everyone in the congregation should treat officers with respect.

"When you lay your head down at night, the policeman is protecting you. And if your car gets stolen, you are going to call the police. If someone breaks into your house, you call the police. What would you do if you had to call the police and there was no answer?"

He said he wasn't diminishing the prestige of his ministry by working with the police, but enhancing it.

"One of the reasons I've joined the Chaplain Corps and united myself with the Police Department is because there's a great deal of misunderstanding and misconception as to how the police and the public protect one another.

"The citizen is an important person, but so is the policeman.

"I've never allowed any of my three children to call a policeman a 'cop' or a 'pig.' To me, that's disrespectful. Such terms indicate that we in the community don't understand the vital importance of police officers.

"You come home and your door is standing open, you're not going to call me. You call a policeman. If you're in any kind of trouble where your life or property may be threatened, you call a policeman.

"The line officer is the difference between anarchy and civilization. How often we forget that. But we're not going to forget it any more in this church, not as far as I'm concerned!"

A chorus of amens and hallelujahs rose from the congregation. And there was wild applause.

After that, Chaplain Barlow had no further opposition to his liaison with the God Squad.

Chaplain Joseph B. Barlow, Jr., stands six feet four inches tall and weighs 231 pounds. A formidable-appearing man with a soft smile, he paid his way through Wayne State University and seminary by fighting as a professional boxer.

Chaplain Barlow is a fervent evangelical, and so are the members of his congregation. "Where Everybody Works Together" is the motto of the church, which has nearly doubled its membership in the last five years because, says Chaplain Barlow, "we really know where God is."

Chaplain Barlow is a man who worries about the high rate of crime among blacks.

"It seems that blacks are involved in more crime than other minority groups or whites," he says. "The main reason is economic. We're a poor people. The black man is still the last to be hired and the first to be fired.

"We also are strongly one-parent. We have a very high percentage of homes in which the husband has left. I know a lot of men who, over a span of eight or ten years, have been involved with three or four different women and have had children with all of them.

"I don't think you are going to change the crime situation among blacks until the home is straightened out. That's one reason the church is so important; we preach the sanctity of the home and marriage.

"You go ahead and build skyscrapers and superhighways and fancy apartment buildings. That's not going to lessen crime. The money has to be spent to create jobs. The focus has to be on the importance of the family working together to make something out of their lives."

Once a boy reaches fourteen, says Chaplain Barlow, the mother is not going to be able to handle him. "You must face that. Society must face that. These children need their fathers."

Asked what can be done to remedy the situation, he replies: "The church is moving to correct some of these abuses. I've managed to bring dozens of fathers back into the home.

"Blacks aren't taught to commit crimes. But it's their poverty, lack of education, and lack of family life that make them into lawbreakers.

"Still, that's not the whole answer. We see white middle-class boys and girls get into serious trouble all the time. Why? Why should they be committing crimes when they've had all the advantages?

"The answer, for black as well as white, is that too many of us have strayed from God."

Most of his spare time, Chaplain Barlow says, is spent with the God Squad. On patrol one evening in southwest Detroit, the squad car in which he was riding answered what promised to be a messy, perhaps dangerous, call. A married couple was engaged in an argument. Both had guns and were threatening to shoot it out with one another.

The officers and Chaplain Barlow arrived at the trim, well-kept house in a few minutes. The chaplain found that the husband and wife were still holding guns aimed at each other. "Both of them smelled of liquor, and there were four frightened children huddled in a corner."

The woman, without being asked, immediately handed her gun to Chaplain Barlow. The man, however, was reluctant to give up his weapon.

"Let's just step into the kitchen for a private talk," Chaplain Barlow said, putting his arm around the man's shoulder.

"I don't want to talk to any minister," the man said, moving the gun upward so that it was pointing at Chaplain Barlow's chest. "I just want to teach my woman a lesson."

"You've got a nice house here," said the chaplain. "And I'm sure that deep down you love your wife and children. I'm sure you work hard. All this could be destroyed in a moment if you fire that gun. You could shoot your wife, or your wife could shoot you. Either way, your children are going to be left without a parent. If you kill her, you're going to jail. If she kills you, she's going to jail."

Praying his reasoning would sink in, Chaplain Barlow let a few seconds tick by.

"Why don't you let us take your guns to the station house," he continued. "You don't need guns in the house. I don't have a gun. I don't carry one, even though I have a permit. Even without a gun, I feel my family is safe and secure and protected."

"It's my Constitutional right to have a gun," the man said.

"That's right. But you've been drinking, and liquor and bullets don't mix. You're not thinking clearly, and you could do something you'll regret for the rest of your life. Prison is no picnic."

The man hesitated for a long moment, then slowly lowered his gun. Chaplain Barlow breathed easier. The man allowed the chaplain to remove the gun from his hand.

Three days later, the man, who earned eight dollars an hour working on a GM assembly line, picked up his two guns at the precinct station house and mailed them to his brother in Alabama.

"I am happy to say," Chaplain Barlow adds, "that the police haven't made a call to that home since that episode occurred, because last May I baptized that man into my church. And I have all his children as members in the church. His wife too."

In the case of John Duggan, Chaplain Barlow, who studied criminology in college, was given the go-ahead by the director of the God Squad to play the role of a detective.

Duggan, a friend of the chaplain's, had come to his office, seeking help. Duggan said he had been arrested and charged with forging a check for $357.

"I wrote some bad checks five years ago," Duggan confessed, "but I swear up and down on the Bible that I didn't write this one."

The chaplain, uncertain whether or not Duggan was telling the truth, decided to investigate. If convicted, Duggan could be sentenced to three years in prison.

Duggan had supplied the chaplain with the names of his friends who'd been with him on the night he supposedly forged the check. Also, the name of the bar where the phony check had been cashed.

Chaplain Barlow sought out Duggan's friends, who denied any knowledge of the forgery. But when the chaplain visited the bartender, he was more talkative.

The bartender said that one of Duggan's friends had lifted a blank check from his pocket and signed his name. The bartender had cashed it.

"But you knew the check was forged," Chaplain Barlow said.

"Duggan was too drunk to sign his own name. I didn't think it mattered."

"But now the bartender was wringing-wet mad," says Chaplain Barlow, "because the check had bounced. He was so angry he reported the forgery to the police."

By the time Duggan's case came to trial, Chaplain Barlow had convinced the bartender to testify. He told the judge what really had happened concerning the forged check, and the charge against Duggan was dropped.

Chaplain Barlow also managed to find justice for one of his parishioners who, while walking in Lincoln Park one night, picked up a white woman. She agreed to let him drive her home.

The parishioner was married, "a well-respected member of the community who unfortunately made a severe error in judgment," says Chaplain Barlow.

On the way to the woman's apartment, the parishioner spotted a police car behind him. He began to speed. The police followed, and a hot pursuit ensued. The chase lasted for nearly half an hour at a speed of eighty-five miles per hour. When the police car finally overtook the racing car, the officers arrested the man.

"When he got out on bail he didn't tell his wife, he told me," says Chaplain Barlow. "The police had thrown the book at him. They charged him with speeding, assault with a deadly vehicle, and resisting arrest."

"Are the charges true?" Chaplain Barlow asked.

"Just the speeding—that's all."

"I don't understand. If you weren't doing anything against the law, why did you start to speed when the police car came up behind you?"

"I didn't want them to catch me with a white woman in my car. I'm from Mississippi. I know what happens if the police catch a black man with a white woman."

In court, Chaplain Barlow, after identifying himself as a member of the Chaplain Corps, became his parishioner's attorney. He told the judge: "There was nothing found in this man's car that justifies the severity of the charges. No narcotics. No gun. No whiskey. This man also has an outstanding driving record. He's never even had a ticket."

"Nevertheless, he was breaking the law," the judge said.

"Judge," Chaplain Barlow answered, "if you were a black man cruising in your car at twelve-thirty at night with a white woman, and the police, who undoubtedly would be white, started chasing you, what would you do?"

"I'd run like the devil," the judge admitted. "I'd do just what this man did."

"Then, Your Honor, I suggest the case be dropped. This man is guilty of speeding only because he was afraid. He denies resisting arrest."

The judge asked the arresting officers if the man, in fact, had resisted arrest. One officer said, "Not exactly." The other added: "Well, he sure didn't want to go to jail."

"I think in this instance the court will be well served by showing leniency," the judge said. "Case dismissed. This isn't Mississippi."

In December 1976, shortly before Christmas, Chaplain Barlow's patrol car responded to a call that involved a bar shooting. When he reached the scene, the chaplain found that four men were dead. Five other patrons were injured. To his horror, as he walked through the carnage, the chaplain discovered that one of the dead men was Samuel Floyd, a young member of his congregation. He had been an innocent bystander.

Three men had entered the bar and attempted to stage a holdup. The bartender wasn't having any of it. From behind the counter, he produced a 30-30 Winchester and began shooting. He killed two of the holdup men; the third escaped and was never apprehended.

The parents of Samuel Floyd were inconsolable. They wept profusely throughout the entire funeral ceremony, which Chaplain Barlow preached. "Naked came I out of my mother's womb, and naked shall I return thither: the Lord gave, and the Lord hath taken away; blessed be the name of the Lord," he quoted from Job 1:21.

Chaplain Barlow called Samuel Floyd's parents into counseling.

"He was only twenty-three years old," Mr. Floyd said. "Too young to die."

"You must thank God for having Samuel for those twenty-three years," Chaplain Barlow responded. He suggested that the parents turn to the Bible for strength. "The earth is the Lord's, and the fulness thereof; the world, and they that dwell therein," Chaplain Barlow read from Psalm 24:1.

Then he said, "People sometimes make the mistake of thinking they own things. But everything on earth, including human life, is the possession of the Lord. Job's ten children were destroyed in one hurricane. Job was rich one night, and he got up the next morning and he was a poor, poor man with all his children dead. But Job persisted. He reconciled himself with God. He didn't lose faith. He said the Lord allowed me the use and pleasure of my children for a number of years. I'm not going to complain.

"The Lord, Mr. and Mrs. Floyd, allowed *you* the pleasure of Samuel for twenty-three years. Thank God for the enjoyment. You must keep on living and striving, as Job did. You've got two other sons, give your affection to them and thank God for them."

Talking in the same vein through several counseling sessions, Chaplain Barlow managed to soothe Samuel Floyd's parents. They accepted their son's death as the will of God. Mr. and Mrs. Floyd, who hadn't been avid churchgoers before, are now among the most committed members of the congregation since Chaplain Barlow led them both to the Lord.

A great tragedy had ended for the Floyds.

A tragedy that has yet to end has occupied the attention of Chaplain Barlow since October 1976.

Officer Julius Donner happened to be standing in line at a bank in East Detroit, waiting to cash his paycheck. He was not on duty. Unexpectedly, the two men in front of him pulled guns on the teller.

Officer Donner acted instinctively. He drew his service revolver and shot and killed one of the robbers. The other, however, wheeled and shot Officer Donner, hitting him in the back of the head above the left ear.

Chaplain Barlow was summoned by God Squad co-ordinator Ed McQueen and went to the hospital. There, he stayed with the parents and the officer's wife.

The doctors emerged with bad news. Julius Donner was alive but unconscious. He was in a coma, and was being kept alive by life-supporting apparatus. The doctors could give his family no date as to when he might awaken from the coma, or if he would live.

"I keep in close touch with the family," says Chaplain Barlow. "I talk with them frequently. And I also go out and visit with them. What do I say to them under such circumstances?" he asks rhetorically. He says he quotes from I Corinthians 13:12, "For now we see through a glass, darkly."

"I tell them there will be a day when we will understand God's vision better. We will understand it bye and bye, like the old Negro spiritual says."

Bye and bye
When the morning comes,
When the mists are rolled away,
We'll understand it all better
Bye and bye.

"Jesus Christ," declares Chaplain Barlow, "is King of Kings and Lord of Lords and when He returns we'll understand why God allows evil to come upon us, why God allows wars to happen, why God allows a good man like Julius Donner to suffer. We don't completely understand it now. We don't have the full answer yet."

Julius Donner's wife, who was pregnant at the time her husband was shot, gave birth to a boy.

Despite what happened to his father, his wife says, "He can be a policeman if he wants to."

The wife and parents of Julius Donner have joined Chaplain Barlow's church, been baptized and accepted the Holy Spirit. Not a day goes by, says the chaplain, when he doesn't pray for Julius Donner, who has yet to awaken from the coma he suffered in October 1976.

CHAPTER 12

Sister Schnell

The big black car, rolling down the quiet street at seventy-five miles an hour, was on a murderous mission. The car, aimed directly at the figure of a woman waiting to cross the street, jumped onto the sidewalk. It swerved sharply toward the woman. She bounded back, barely in time, her life saved by inches.

There is danger in the streets of Detroit even for a nun. The assassination vehicle had meant to take the life of Sister Francis Winifred Schnell, a Dominican nun who became the second female member of the God Squad in 1974 and appears to be a woman who has never had an enemy in her life.

Dressed in a smart blue suit and blue blouse, with a large silver cross hanging from her neck, she was one of the last nuns in her order to give up the habit—"though I'm going to be buried in it."

Born in Detroit, she seems much younger than fifty-four. She has clean, chiseled, well-scrubbed features and perfect white teeth, lodged in a round face that is usually smiling.

She's a "police brat." Her father joined the Department in 1907 and was the first officer to ride in a patrol car. He eventually became an inspector, and at his retirement, after twenty-eight years on the force, was head of the vice squad.

Sister Schnell grew up on police stories. "In fact, when I was only six or seven years old, Dad would take me along when he staged raids on gambling joints or in the Cass Corridor red-light district. I'd sit in the back of the car while he staked the establishment out. Then he'd go into a bar and make a call to headquarters, ordering the place to be hit.

"He used to take me down to the station house and the officers would pick me up, put me on the counter, and spoil me terribly by giving me candy."

Sister Schnell was an elementary and high school teacher in Catholic schools for twenty-five years. When the last school in which she taught closed because of a lack of funds and enrollment, she became a secretary at Detroit's Harbor Hospital, where she is paid $600 a month.

She says candidly she doesn't particularly enjoy her job "because it's mostly office work. I like being with people. That's one of the main reasons I joined the Corps.

"My idea of the Corps is to serve and give care to police officers and their families and to do what I can to help the community at large, particularly the impoverished."

Sister Schnell says she's made runs in squad cars a number of times, "but normally that isn't my function."

While she was still in training, the patrol car in which she was riding became involved in chasing down a robbery suspect. "We caught him, but the officers radioed for another car to take me back to the precinct because they didn't want me to share the back seat with a criminal. The Lord knows, he might have been a strayed Catholic, and if I could have talked to him perhaps I could have done something about that. But the officers were a little protective of me at first."

Early in her God Squad career, Chaplain Schnell received a phone call at three in the afternoon from Bill Paris, asking her to report to Detroit General Hospital. The fourteen-year-old son of a detective had apparently attempted to commit suicide.

But the boy's father, a veteran policeman, told Chaplain Schnell shortly after she arrived: "It was an accident. He was just cleaning one of my guns and it went off."

To this day, says Chaplain Schnell, no one knows if it was an accident or a try at suicide. "But I give the officer the benefit of the doubt. I tend to believe it *was* an accident. I know these things happen, but I still think it impossible that a child of fourteen would attempt to take his own life, no matter what the circumstances."

Chaplain Schnell spent twenty-two hours in the hospital waiting room with the boy's father and mother. The doctors' prognosis wasn't optimistic—they said they didn't expect the young man to live. The doctors said it was too risky to attempt to remove the bullet, which was nested in the lower portion of the boy's neck. At midnight, however, the boy was taken into surgery again. This time the bullet was removed. But his lungs had collapsed. His right side and left arm were paralyzed. His speech was impaired, and the doctors didn't know whether or not his kidneys would function. They had him on a catheter.

The mother, says Chaplain Schnell, was taking it hard. "She was almost a basket case, and the doctors had to give her medication to quiet her down.

"I tried to explain to her that God had a reason for the accident, and we prayed together. After a while, she more or less accepted it.

"In an emotionally explosive situation like that, where a life is hanging in the balance, there isn't too much you can say, because people are in no condition to be responsive."

By the grace of God, says Chaplain Schnell, the boy rallied the next day and the doctors said he would pull through.

The boy had a slow recovery—he spent three and a half months in the hospital.

"Now, when I'm over to the house, I see him in the backyard running around and playing a little football. The only reminder of his wound is a slight paralysis in his right hand and the fact that his condition is too medically uncertain for him to return to school."

Chaplain Schnell felt that her job hadn't ended with the boy's discharge from the hospital. From conversations she'd had with the parents, she knew counseling was necessary, especially for the mother.

For one thing, now that her son was home, the mother was overprotecting him. She babied him, gave him everything he wanted, "which didn't do much to make him self-sufficient," notes the chaplain.

The mother also blamed her husband for the accident. If the husband hadn't been on the force and hadn't had guns in the house, it never would have happened. In addition, the mother was jealous of her husband because the bulk of their son's attention was directed toward the father. The boy idolized his father and wanted to be a policeman too. Now the mother was grateful in a way for the accident because her son's partial paralysis would prevent him from qualifying for the force. "One policeman in the family is enough," the mother said.

Chaplain Schnell worked with the mother for more than a year. "She wasn't a terribly attractive woman. She had a terrible case of psoriasis. I got her to go to the doctor for that, and it's pretty well cleared up now. I worked with her on her grooming, because she was unkempt in her dress and hair style. She'd just let herself go.

"I told her stories about how my dad had often been gone from home for long periods and the many, many nights he missed his dinner because he was busy with police business. That seemed to mitigate her jealousy of her husband's job."

The family relationship is much better now, says Chaplain Schnell.

"I think the accident drove the husband and wife closer together, made them appreciate their son more, because they nearly lost him.

"I had a series of talks with the husband, urging him to spend as much time at home as possible. The Detroit Police Department wasn't the only thing in life.

"Now he's found ways to spend more time with his wife and son. I think the son will be back in school soon and he's almost good as new.

"So you might say the accident was a blessing in disguise. They are now a happy family. They're always asking me over. I go over there as often as I can for supper. They think of me as one of the family. It's beautiful."

Chaplain Schnell also came to the aid of another jealous policeman's wife. The couple had two sons, six and eight. The wife felt that her husband wasn't giving his family the love and affection they needed. After she put the children to bed she was alone, really alone, the wife told Chaplain Schnell, because her husband worked the midnight-to-eight shift.

After several meetings with the mother, Chaplain Schnell found that she was mostly feeling sorry for herself. Her real problem was that she wasn't actively engaged in the community. She wasn't doing anything except taking care of the children and arguing with her husband about his job.

Chaplain Schnell thinks there ought to be a program in the Police Department—and maybe the Corps should initiate it—in which the wives go out with their husbands on patrol duty in order to see how dangerous their jobs are. "My heart goes out to police officers, because their lives are on the line every time they leave their homes. And to come back home to a picky wife, that is kind of hard to take."

As a result of counseling, Chaplain Schnell got the wife to help out in her sons' school, serving lunch in the cafeteria. Then, on her own, the wife volunteered for playground duty. Now she is in a host of other volunteer activities as well.

Chaplain Schnell also convinced the officer to switch shifts occasionally with a buddy, so he and his wife could go out a couple of times a month. Chaplain Schnell describes them as a reconciled, happy couple now.

"If I saved a marriage, the Lord only knows. A lot of it was caused by the unthinking selfishness of the wife, which is all too typical of many police wives who get jealous of their husband's jobs.

"I wouldn't want to be a policeman's wife, never. I don't think I could cope with it, never knowing when he left the house if he'd be home or not. A woman has to have attention, affection, and love, and a lot of times it doesn't work that way."

Every Friday, Sister Schnell receives a list from her 7th Precinct commander with the names of officers who are sick or disabled. No matter what faith they are, she calls them. She's the only chaplain on the God Squad who conducts this type of telephone ministry.

"It's beautiful how the officers will say, 'Well, this has never happened before. How come you are calling me?' One officer I was talking with the other night—he's only thirty years old and unmarried—was telling me he'd been in a freak motorcycle accident. He had mounted his cycle and was ready to take off when his windshield inexplicably flew up and threw him. He has a bad back problem, and he's been off duty for more than a year."

Once a month there is a community meeting at the 7th Precinct. "I always go," says the chaplain, "because I feel it's very important for someone from the Corps to work with the people of the community to help improve relationships between them and the Police Department."

Citizens who attend the community meetings give Chaplain Schnell the names of people who are ill. Also of shut-ins, and some who haven't been out of their apartments in months.

"Then I go into the inner city and visit them. I like working in the inner city. You are out among the people, dealing with those who are the poorest of the poor, people just living on a tiny Social Security check, welfare, or ADC. These are women who have several children, but no husbands."

Mostly, says Chaplain Schnell, the work is listening. "They're struggling so terribly hard. It's letting them know that someone cares, no matter who they are and no matter how little they have.

"What is really beautiful is that the women on ADC love their children. And if they have parents, they never put them in a nursing home. No matter how poor they are, they will keep their parents at home. The parents may not get very many material things, but they get love."

Chaplain Schnell recalls a woman in her thirties who had six children, was divorced and on ADC.

"She always looked lovely, and so did the kids. But their home, well, it was indescribable. The steps of the porch were all broken, and on one visit, there to greet me at the front door was a huge dead rat. I just kicked it aside, even though I was horrified."

The chaplain says the children, who ranged in age from six to eighteen, were extremely well-behaved. "But they had four dogs who did their duty right on the floor. You had to step gently to avoid the dogs' puddles. The mattresses on the floor were filthy.

Their bedroom clothes were piled up in a corner, stacked to the ceiling."

Yet, says the chaplain, the family was immaculate, with never an odor about them. "I was there to arrange the enrollment of the children in school, which I managed to do."

The mother was Catholic, though not practicing. The church in that area, according to the chaplain, isn't geared to take care of the black community. It's primarily a white church whose congregation is made up of Belgian-Americans. About two hundred of them travel in from the suburbs each Sunday to attend the church. Most fled to the suburbs after the 1967 riot, abandoning the community to the blacks.

"They come back every week for Mass," the chaplain says, "because it is their church. I know that blacks don't feel it's theirs. That's why a lot of them never go."

As for the family, says the chaplain, they finally moved out of the parish.

"The mother finished high school, and I encouraged her to go to secretarial school at night. She had the fortitude to go through with it. She also had the fortitude to keep her family together. The last I heard she had a pretty good paying job as a secretary and was off ADC."

The widow of a police officer who'd been gunned down in a finance-company robbery called Chaplain Schnell not long ago, asking for counseling for her daughter, who was pregnant and unmarried. Could Chaplain Schnell convince her daughter to give up the child for adoption after it was born?

Chaplain Schnell met with the seventeen-year-old girl, who told her firmly that she not only intended to have the child but didn't want to give it up, no matter what her mother said. The girl said she would get a job and support her baby.

"I was more on the side of the girl," says Chaplain Schnell, "because I don't feel that a mother should give up a child, even if it is illegitimate. If there's enough love there and the mother feels she can take care of it, it's better for her to keep the child."

Chaplain Schnell went to the girl's mother with a single mission in mind—to convince her to accept her grandchild.

"If my daughter insists on keeping the child, they can't live in this house," the mother said stubbornly.

"In that case," Chaplain Schnell replied, "I'll have your daughter and grandchild move into my apartment, small as it is."

Presented with that threat, the mother gradually gave in.

When the baby was born, says the chaplain, the change that came over the grandmother was amazing.

"She thinks there isn't another child in all the world as beautiful as her grandson."

She takes care of him all day while her daughter works as a waitress.

"I see the three of them in church regularly. They are a happy, well-adjusted family now. Out of crisis came love—and you can't ask much more in this world."

Chaplain Schnell is nothing if not courageous. She's made of stern stuff, a true-grit nun unafraid of a fight. She proved it a few years ago when a band of Black Panthers opened a headquarters next door to the church where her convent was located.

"From my window I could look into their place and see posters of all these Communist leaders on the walls: Lenin, Stalin, and Mao Tse-tung. That got my Irish up. I went over there one Sunday morning, the door happened to be unlocked, and I tore the posters off the wall."

The next day there was a threatening letter from the Panthers in Chaplain Schnell's mailbox. It said they knew she had ripped the posters from the walls. The posters were expensive and she had to pay to replace them. Otherwise, the Panthers added, they were going to have her for dinner.

When she refused, the next Panther move was an attempt to set the convent on fire. The smoldering blaze in the convent's kitchen was discovered and put out before it did any serious damage. Then, a few days later, the convent was invaded again and the telephone torn off the wall. Following that vandalism, the Panthers went after Chaplain Schnell in a big black car, attempting to run her down on a quiet street near the convent.

"They were really angry at me," says Chaplain Schnell. "But I'm not the type to be scared."

Next, the Panthers staged a march around the church, with signs calling for Chaplain Schnell to leave the community. When that failed to budge her, the Panthers called a meeting at their headquarters. An overflow crowd of more than one hundred people in the neighborhood showed up to consider the question of whether or not Chaplain Schnell was still a welcome member of the community.

The Panthers charged Chaplain Schnell with being a spy for the police. They also said she was a racist who hated all blacks.

The verdict appeared to be going against her until a tall black man in his early twenties rose and told his story. He said that when he was arrested for using narcotics, Chaplain Schnell had come to his aid. He'd been a heroin addict, and the chaplain had gone with him to the clinic whenever he needed methadone. Then, through prayer and counseling, the chaplain had helped him rid himself of his heroin habit altogether! "She saved my life," he concluded.

"It was so beautiful," says Chaplain Schnell. "I didn't even know Roger was going to be there or that he'd talk about our working together to rid him of heroin. After he finished speaking, I couldn't help but cry."

There was a voice vote, and almost unanimously Chaplain Schnell was invited to remain in the community. A week later, the Black Panthers moved out and haven't been back since.

CHAPTER 13

Notice in a Bank Window

"We've got a jumper!"

The call came from a police lieutenant to Father John Nader, one of the founding members of the God Squad.

"We can't talk him down, Father. Maybe you can," the lieutenant said.

"Where is he?"

"On the roof of the Camelot Hotel."

Father Nader slammed the phone down, and from his base at twin-domed St. Mary's church in downtown Detroit, he reached the hotel in less than ten minutes.

There was already a crowd, a battery of police officers, firemen with a wide net, and an ambulance. A phone crew was busy running a special line to the roof.

In briefing Father Nader, a deputy inspector said: "The jumper says he won't go over if he can make a telephone call to his mother."

Father Nader took the elevator to the eleventh floor, then walked a flight of stairs to the roof. Perched near the edge was a short, dark man who readily told the chaplain that his name was Luis Chacon, and that he was a Mexican-American from Amarillo, Texas.

It was a hot summer night in July, and though Chacon didn't allow Chaplain Nader to come within ten feet of him, the clergyman could smell the beer on Chacon's breath.

When Chaplain Nader asked Chacon what was troubling him, he replied: "I can't find work. I'm on welfare. I've called my mother in

Amarillo a couple of times collect, but she won't accept the charges and talk to me. What is there to live for?"

"How old are you?"

"Twenty-five."

"You've answered your own question—everything in life is before you."

"No, my life is a mess. Nobody wants me. Nobody loves me."

"We'll try to reach your mother. We'll try to get you a job. Only, don't do anything foolish."

Chacon suddenly turned angry when the sound of a fire engine pierced the air.

"The fire engine's coming for me," Chacon said, putting one foot over the ledge. "They think they're going to run a ladder up here and get me."

Chaplain Nader explained calmly that the fire engine undoubtedly was only responding to a call. "But there are a lot of people vitally interested in saving your life."

"Why?"

"The Lord considers every life, every soul, as precious. Are you Catholic?"

"Yes, and I go to church most Sundays."

"Then, you know that the Lord counts what you're threatening to do as a sin. Why don't you come over here? We'll walk downstairs and have a cup of coffee and talk it over."

"No. I want to talk to my mother."

At that moment, a telephone company employee, trailing a long cord behind him, appeared on the roof. "We've got a connection," he said, handing the phone to Chaplain Nader.

Chacon gave the chaplain his mother's number in Amarillo. The chaplain dialed the number and let the phone ring for long minutes. But there was no answer.

"I'm sorry," the chaplain said. "It looks like your mother isn't home. We can try again later."

"She's home. She just isn't answering the phone because she knows it's me. I've been trying to talk to her for two days. What kind of mother refuses to even talk with her son on the telephone?"

"Why don't you try making the call yourself?"

Chacon agreed, removing his leg from the ledge. "You put the phone down and back up," Chacon said. "You try anything and I'll jump."

Chaplain Nader obeyed instructions, backing up about fifteen feet.

In order to place the call, Chacon had to walk to the center of the roof. The line only stretched that far.

Chacon took the phone in hand and, as he began to dial, Chaplain Nader and a sergeant who materialized, seemingly from nowhere, grabbed him. Both the priest and the policeman made flying tackles, flooring and capturing Chacon. The sergeant had been hidden on the roof in the elevator housing, a small shedlike building which contained the elevator's motor.

Chacon was sent to Detroit General Hospital for three days of psychiatric examination and released.

"The case made the papers," Chaplain Nader says, "and we were flooded with job offers for him. A particularly good offer at good pay came in from Chrysler. There were also job offers from as far away as Texas."

After he was released from the hospital, Chacon met with Father Nader at his office in St. Mary's.

His head hung down, Chacon said: "I want to thank you for saving my life. You were right, it was a foolish thing to do."

Chacon said he had talked with his mother several times and decided to go home. Chaplain Nader bought his plane ticket.

"I still hear from him occasionally," says Chaplain Nader. "Luis is married now, has a child, and is working happily as a mechanic. He is completely reconciled with his mother. What happened at the Camelot Hotel two years ago is only a memory."

One tragic footnote to the case involved the sergeant who had helped Chaplain Nader subdue Chacon on the roof. Says the chaplain: "When the sergeant jumped, he landed on his heel and broke it. As a matter of fact, he had to give up his career because of that injury."

Father John Nader, relaxing in his spacious St. Mary's office in a huge red-brick church complete with a lovely grotto, says, "I was born four blocks from here in 1924."

He doesn't look like a man who should be tackling people on the roofs of eleven-story hotels. He's short, five feet six inches, and weighs 190 pounds. He stares out at the world from merry brown eyes and counts himself fortunate in that he has a "steady" congregation of about four hundred registered parishioners. "We're holding our own quite nicely," he says.

Even before there was a God Squad, Father Nader was working with the Police Department as a chaplain. His duties then were less eventful, confined to benedictions at departmental dinners, appearances at various Police Department ceremonies, especially when citations for bravery and promotions were awarded . . . and attending funerals of police officers. "There have been so many police funerals. I hope there's never another one."

Father Nader says: "Of course we changed quite dramatically in 1973 when Bill Paris, myself, and a few other ministers came up with this Corps concept. The Corps was an outgrowth of a lot of things, particularly of the 1967 riot and the feeling of the black community that it wasn't getting a fair shake from a predominantly white Police Department.

"I think it's worked out very well. I would recommend that a Chaplain Corps, which functions as we do, become part of every police department in the country."

Of all the God Squad incidents in which he's been involved, the one that stands out in Chaplain Nader's mind is the death of Officer William Casey, because of its brutality and because of the strength exhibited by his widow.

Officer Casey was with one of his sons, performing an errand at a bank in downtown Detroit for his wife. He was off duty. Shortly after he entered the bank, two holdup men walked in and ordered everyone to freeze.

Instead, Officer Casey shoved his son out of the way, removed his service revolver and fired. He missed, but the robbers didn't. They pumped three bullets into him and he fell bleeding to the floor.

"It was a very, very brutal shooting," says Father Nader.

Officer Casey was sped by ambulance to Carmel Hospital and rushed into surgery.

Alerted to the incident by Officer Casey's commander, Chaplain Nader darted to the hospital, where he met the policeman's wife.

"Despite the fact that her husband was close to death, she was in command of herself. There were tears, but she didn't break down like the wives of so many other wounded officers that I've seen. She said she'd like to go to the chapel at St. Mary's and pray, which we did."

By the time they got back to the hospital, Officer Casey was dead. He'd died on the operating table.

"She's managed quite well since her husband's death," Chaplain Nader says. "There are five children. The only way I can describe her is to say that she's got fantastic strength, tremendous strength.

"She calls me occasionally and we talk. Though her husband's been dead for three years, she's given no thought to remarriage. She just tends to her business, raising her children in a good, decent, Christian home. She considers the loss of her husband a private affair and never speaks of it."

Once a year, on September 8, the anniversary of the holdup, the bank inserts a notice, bordered in heavy black lead, in its window and in the Detroit newspapers. "The notice," says Chaplain Nader, "expresses the bank's continuing appreciation for Officer Casey, what he stood for, what the Police Department stands for, and what Officer Casey did. It's really a tribute to the entire Department."

Otherwise, except for Chaplain Nader and Officer Casey's family, no one remembers the blue-eyed, redheaded Irish policeman who forfeited his life at the age of thirty-four. His killers have never been caught.

CHAPTER 14

The Difference

He walks in Bill Paris' shoes.

Reverend William Crenshaw, who succeeded the slain chaplain as executive director of the God Squad, is fifty-eight years old, an enormously likable man who is pastor of a 700-member all-black Christian Methodist Episcopal congregation in the heart of the inner city.

At this moment his brown eyes are alive with anger.

"Someone broke into my church last night," he says, unable yet to quite comprehend what he calls an outrage.

The thieves hammered in the doors, breaking them apart to gain entrance. They stole an IBM typewriter and a Royal adding machine. The contents of the filing cabinets in the church office were dumped to the floor, and the Sunday school was vandalized.

"They were looking for money, but I keep no money in our building. What they did is like robbing the poor box—that's the lowest crime there is in the sight of God.

"Nothing is sacred any more, nothing, even a church. There was a time when we didn't even have keys to the church. When I came to Detroit eighteen years ago, the doors of the church were kept open all the time. Now we have to lock up and board up to protect our property."

Reverend Crenshaw says that $1,500, which could go to a better cause, has been earmarked from the church budget for the installation of a burglar-alarm system.

As both the pastor of a large congregation ("Our attendance is picking up Sunday after Sunday") and chief of the Chaplain Corps, his days are crowded and eventful.

"I take my responsibility to the Corps very, very seriously," Chaplain Crenshaw says. "After all, I replaced a man who really couldn't be replaced."

Married for thirty-three years, he has two daughters. A solidly built man who weighs two hundred pounds, he is five feet nine and a half inches tall. Yet he is a giant in Detroit, a peripatetic minister with a mission.

"That mission, simply, is to make certain the Corps is run efficiently and effectively."

Like Bill Paris and other members of the God Squad, Chaplain Crenshaw has been confronted with a barricaded-gunman incident.

Recently, on the lower west side of the city, a thirty-five-year-old man had beaten his common-law wife and was holding her and their five children captive.

When Chaplain Crenshaw arrived at the scene, officers had set up telephone communication with the man.

Chaplain Crenshaw, prepared to go into the house if necessary, got on the phone and talked nonstop with the man for two hours. He said he had a rifle and a pistol. "I know you want to kill me, but if anyone breaks down the door they are dead."

At first, says Chaplain Crenshaw, the man spouted "a whole lot of off-the-wall stuff. He sounded half drunk and he wasn't making sense."

Gradually, Chaplain Crenshaw began to win the man's confidence. He was calming down, his anger dissipating.

A short time later, the man asked for prayer.

Chaplain Crenshaw quoted from Psalm 23 ("The Lord is my shepherd; I shall not want . . .") and John 14:1–2 ("Let not your heart be troubled: ye believe in God, believe also in me. In my Father's house are many mansions: if it were not so, I would have told you. I go to prepare a place for you.").

After the prayer, the man meekly walked out of the house, followed by his mangled wife and frightened children. It turned out that the man had not had any weapons.

Chaplain Crenshaw says the man "couldn't believe I was a

minister who was working with the Police Department. As for his wife, it was just a pitiful sight. He had beaten her eyes blue, and there were bruises all over her face, neck, and shoulders."

What had triggered the incident?

"His wife said that the only way he could satisfy himself sexually was to whip her before they made love. That's some kind of strange lovemaking. Sick."

The wife was sent to the hospital and the man was arrested. A judge ordered him confined to a psychiatric institution for a week's observation.

After the incident, Chaplain Crenshaw worked tirelessly with the couple. His efforts brought the type of results that are counted in heaven. The man and his wife were led to the Lord by Chaplain Crenshaw and they joined his church. "They tell me their sex life is normal now, and he no longer beats his wife," the chaplain adds.

The saddest calls to answer, says Chaplain Crenshaw, are those that involve a policeman being shot.

In March 1977, the chaplain, while riding in a patrol car, heard on the radio that an officer had been critically wounded by a prowler.

"Since I was on the street that night, I made the hospital call," the chaplain says. "The officer was dead by the time I got there."

His wife was screaming, "He left the house two hours ago alive and well."

Chaplain Crenshaw put his arm around the woman's shoulders and uttered an extemporaneous prayer: "We ask you, God, for blessings on this officer and his wife. Help her to understand that her loss is not in vain. That her husband was trying to protect human life and society. Show her, dear God, wisdom and mercy and understanding and the peace that passes all understanding."

The chaplain says that at a time of crisis the color line disappears.

"Here I was, a black man, with my arm around a white police widow. But she didn't care if I was black or white or green. And she didn't care about denomination, whether I was a Jew or Gentile or Buddhist.

"At the point of severe impact, people want consolation, and it doesn't matter who you are or what you are as long as you are there to help."

Chaplain Crenshaw has talked with the widow a number of times. "She still hasn't fully adjusted to her husband's death, but God is working on her spirit. Pretty soon, I'm certain He will give her the serenity that will enable her to go on to lead a normal life."

Patrol-car duty occasionally has its lighter moments. One night while riding in a squad car, Chaplain Crenshaw and the two officers with him saw a man running naked along a downtown street.

"We all got out of the car and started chasing him. I was huffing and puffing when we caught up to him after five blocks. There wasn't much to it. The fellow merely looked foolish. He was just drunk, soaked up."

But then there are the nights in the patrol car when the action is more exciting.

On one such evening the two white officers with whom Chaplain Crenshaw was riding spotted a black teen-ager at the wheel of a stolen car.

A high-speed pursuit ensued, with the driver eluding the police car for about fifteen minutes. He finally came to a halt in a residential area, hopped out and ran into a house. The officers and Chaplain Crenshaw followed him into the house, and he was captured.

"Right away, his mother started shouting, 'Police brutality!'" says the chaplain.

She said, "The only reason these white officers are arresting my son is because he's black."

Chaplain Crenshaw told the woman that her son was driving a stolen car, which at the moment was parked in front of her own house. Instead of creating a disturbance or causing trouble, she had best get her son a bail bondsman. The woman, however, refused to believe that her son had stolen a car.

Subsequently she wrote a bristling letter to the chief of police with her charges of police brutality.

"She wrote that letter even in the face of the evidence of the stolen car. It was ridiculous. I informed the chief that there had been no brutality and that the officers had even risked their lives in the high-speed chase. And that ended that."

Chaplain Crenshaw says he isn't afraid when he's riding patrol.

"If I were afraid, I wouldn't do it. I am not afraid because I believe firmly that riding in the patrol cars is an extension of my ministerial calling. I don't believe that my work is housed between four walls. I think my work encompasses more than being a minister of the gospel. And then, there's always a silent partner, a fourth person riding in that car with you . . . God . . .

"If there's any fear at all, it comes later, when you think of what might have happened, like this car chase I was just talking about. We were doing seventy, eighty, ninety miles an hour, with the sirens going and the red lights flashing, and anything, a crash or some type of accident, could have occurred. But at the time you have no fear."

Another reason Chaplain Crenshaw is fearless, he says, is because he's accustomed to police work. When he was discharged from the Army after World War II, he worked as a police officer in Louisville, Kentucky, for five years while he was attending seminary.

"So naturally I've got a soft spot in my heart for law-enforcement people."

Thus, the chaplain considers the suicide of a police officer a particular waste and a needless tragedy.

"If we could get to them in time, I'm sure the members of the Corps could prevent any policeman from killing himself."

He recalls the suicide of one officer several years ago and attending the funeral with Bill Paris.

The officer was divorced. His wife had left him, taking their two children. He became despondent, and apparently that's why he took his life.

A few days after the funeral, Chaplain Crenshaw and Bill Paris visited the widow, offering their services.

"But she was something of a disappointment to us as a human being," says Chaplain Crenshaw. "She didn't seem too broken up about her ex-husband's death now. Yet, at the funeral she carried on worse than anybody. They practically had to carry her in and out of the cemetery."

On several occasions, says Chaplain Crenshaw, he's been able to intercede and save the jobs of policemen.

He worked with one officer for three months. Together, Chaplain

Crenshaw and the policeman gradually found common ground and were able to identify the problem. The officer had recently killed two men in the line of duty, and was now afraid of carrying a gun.

"Once that was determined," says Chaplain Crenshaw, "the solution was quite simple. I explained the situation to his commander, and the officer was transferred from the street to the communications section."

In another counseling case, a policeman's wife accused her husband of having more than a professional interest in the woman officer who was his partner.

Chaplain Crenshaw talked to the policewoman and found that she was happily married and had two children. She was upset at the charge, feeling her job might be in jeopardy.

"I went back to the wife and told her that her suspicions were groundless. Her husband was faithful. She seemed quite relieved that I'd taken the trouble to investigate the policewoman. Things were patched up in fine shape between them. I finally got the situation worked out to where they both joined my church."

But, the chaplain adds, there have been problems on the force since women officers started riding in patrol cars. There have even been instances where two male officers will argue about who is going to ride with a particular female officer. "But we're seeing less and less of that sort of thing."

Working on the attitudes of policemen is as important as riding in the patrol cars, Chaplain Crenshaw says.

"I don't care how good a police department you have—and we have a very good one—there are going to be some officers that don't come up to par. There are going to be some that are prejudiced."

One night on patrol duty, Chaplain Crenshaw was riding with a white officer who came from Virginia.

Every time he'd stop a black man he'd call him "nigger."

The chaplain called the officer aside and candidly warned him that if he didn't stop using the racial slur he would recommend that he be taken off the street, perhaps fired.

"Every man is equal," I told him. "You must treat blacks and whites like human beings. A man is a human being before he is a black man or a white man. And you have to recognize that."

Unfortunately, the officer from Virginia persisted in his attitude, and he was eventually separated from the force.

"We don't have too many cases like that any more," says Chaplain Crenshaw. "It's much, much better than it used to be. In large part, that's because of the existence of the Corps."

Asked to sum up the Corps and what difference the God Squad has made in Detroit, Chaplain Crenshaw replies:

"What difference have we made? I think we have made a lot of difference. I've heard countless policemen and citizens say they feel a new sense of security because of us. They say it's an inspiration to see Christian ministers fighting crime and helping in so many other ways in police work.

"The city is very pleased with what the Corps is doing.

"And when you speak of the Corps, remember you are talking about Bill Paris' monument. It's also the living monument of every man and woman in the Corps.

"There's a vast difference between working as an average pastor, out of the line of fire, and working for the Corps.

"This Corps, this God Squad, is vivid testimony to the fact that God cares, that God is out there on the streets of Detroit crying out for men to abandon sin and abide with Him.

"The Corps is an active, concerned, involved instrument of God.

"It's the sword and the Bible, the good, decent, dedicated right hand of the Lord."